Friendship

REVISIONS

A Series of Books on Ethics

General Editors:
Stanley Hauerwas and Alasdair MacIntyre

We are too often in our contemporary ethical debates and disagreements the prisoners of an unrecognized moral history. The fragmentation of a complex past— Jewish, Catholic, Aristotelian, Puritan, Humanist and more—has left us as the warring heirs of an inadequate inheritance. So our disagreements are all too easily framed as a series of encounters between abstract and unreal stereotypes in which a rootless liberalism is counterposed to a reactionary conservatism. In this situation the dominant modes of recent ethical writing, whether philosophical or theological, are often unhelpful. They encourage us to lapse once more either into unhistorical abstractions or the unargued dogmatism surrounding discussion of concrete moral issues. This series marks an attempt to recover what is viable in the traditions of which we ought to be the heirs without ignoring what it was that made those traditions vulnerable to modernity.

Friendship

A Study in Theological Ethics

GILBERT MEILAENDER

UNIVERSITY OF NOTRE DAME PRESS
NOTRE DAME   LONDON

241. 676
M

Library of Congress Cataloging in Publication Data

Meilaender, Gilbert, 1946-
    Friendship, a study in theological ethics.
    (Revisions ; v. 2)
      1. Friendship.   I. Title.   II. Series.
    Revisions (University of Notre Dame) ; v. 2
    BJ1533.F8M36   241'.676   81-50459
    ISBN 0-268-00956-2   AACR2

Manufactured in the United States of America

TO JUDY

"A friend or companion is always welcome,
but better still to be husband and wife."

Contents

Acknowledgments

To acknowledge debts to one's friends is always a joy. To acknowledge debts to some friends and not to others adds risk to joy. Here I confine myself to only a few of my most obvious debts. Some of my first reading and thinking about friendship was done with the aid of a summer research grant from the University of Virginia (and friendly conversations with many colleagues there) and continued with the aid of a summer grant from Oberlin College.

I have little doubt, to journey farther into my past, that my interest in the problem of special moral relations—if not the focus on friendship—comes from two men who were my teachers and, though still my teachers, are also my friends: Gene Outka and Paul Ramsey. Those who know their writings will realize that neither is likely to agree fully with what I have to say, but their influence has been deeply felt. In addition, Paul Ramsey has encouraged me in the writing of this manuscript, has criticized it with the usual zest he brings to such work, and—most important to me—has shaped my conception of the task of theological ethics.

Stanley Hauerwas's reading and evaluation of the manuscript greatly encouraged me. And, a different sort of debt, I must thank my sister Marion whose vastly superior knowledge of the French language made available to me some of the riches of L. Dugas's famous work on friendship.

ix

Other special moral relations, not just friendship, are important in one's life, and I am continually grateful for the richness Peter, Ellen, and Hannah add to life and the claims they make on me.

Montaigne, in his justly famous essay on friendship, expressed the view that the soul of women is not "firm enough to support the strain of so hard and durable a knot" as friendship. Nevertheless, he allowed himself to speculate that "if such a free and voluntary familiarity could be established, where not only the souls might have their complete enjoyment, but the bodies also shared in the alliance, in which the entire man was engaged, it is certain that the friendship would be the fuller and more perfect." The dedication of this book expresses my belief that in this speculation, at least, Montaigne was not mistaken.

Prologue

"When friendships were the noblest things in the world, charity was little," Jeremy Taylor wrote, pointing thereby to an important historical shift in the culture of the West.[1] There can be little doubt that friendship was a considerably more important topic in the life and thought of the classical civilizations of Greece and Rome than it has, for the most part, been within Christendom. With the possible exception of the literature of monasticism, friendship has never been a central concern of Christian thought. By contrast, Aristotle devoted two of the ten books of his *Nicomachean Ethics* to friendship. It would be difficult, if not impossible, to find a contemporary ethicist—whether philosophical or theological—who in writing a basic introduction to ethics would give friendship more than a passing glance. Indeed, having been for a time in the modern period the province of essayists (such as Emerson), friendship now appears to have fallen to a still lower estate: A book on friendship now means, quite often, a collection of little sayings, attractively illustrated, meant as a gift, and sold in a drug store.

The reasons for this are no doubt many. Ours is a world in which work has become dominant, and we identify ourselves in terms of what we do (for pay), not who our friends are. Aristotle says, alluding it seems to a Greek proverb, that friends must have eaten the required pinch of salt together—that is, spent a good bit of time in each other's company. And in a world in which work has become dominant, that becomes more

1

difficult as mobility becomes more necessary and com-
monplace. We do not have to be fascinated with "roots"
in order to realize that an essential prerequisite for
friendship—time spent together—may be lacking in our
world. Then too, in our culture the erotic relationship
between a man and a woman—crowned at one time, if
no longer, in Christian marriage—became the bond of
love in which people invested themselves most deeply.
Indeed, that relationship has been subjected to as much
ethical scrutiny within Christendom as friendship was
within the ancient world of Greece and Rome. Furthermore, ethics as we have understood it since the time of
Kant, and then Mill, has been concerned primarily with
our obligations, not with the many choices we make
about how we will live. And friendship, a personal bond
entered freely and without obligation, has been unable
to find a place in ethics so conceived.

When these and whatever other good reasons there
are for the decline of friendship have been adduced,
however, we must also add another, specifically theological, consideration. "When friendships were the
noblest things in the world, charity was little," and if
the bond of friendship lost its pride of place it is partly
because the roots of Christian culture go very deep into
a man who is reported to have said: "If you love those
who love you, what reward have you?. . . And if you
salute only your brethren, what more are you doing
than others?" (Matthew 5:46f.). Within Christian
thought *agape* displaced *philia*, and it is impossible to
think theologically about love without giving that
simple fact careful consideration.[2] Although the early
Christians did use the term "friends of God" (*philoi
tou theou*) as a self-designation referring to all Christians, it seems that they did not refer to one another as
"friends" but, instead, as "brethren"—a term which,
Harnack hypothesizes, they may have thought even
more "inward and warm."[3]

The theological motivation for this displacement is not hard to find, and the chapters of this book will explore some aspects of it. Philia is clearly a preferential bond in which we are drawn by what is attractive or choiceworthy in the friend; agape is to be nonpreferential, like the love of the Father in heaven who makes his sun rise on the evil and the good and sends rain on the just and the unjust (Matthew 5:45). Philia is, in addition, a mutual bond, marked by the inner reciprocities of love; agape is to be shown even to the enemy, who, of course, cannot be expected to return such love. Philia is recognized to be subject to change; agape is to be characterized by the same fidelity which God shows to his covenant. Philia was the noblest thing in the world in an age when "civic friendship" was a widely shared ideal; agape has dominated our understanding of love in a world in which the sphere of politics has been desacralized by the search of the restless heart for a suprahistorical resting place in God. Philia was the preeminent bond in a world for which work was of relatively little personal significance; agape helped shape a world in which vocation was seen as a supremely important form of service to the neighbor.

Those five contrasts form the central matter of the chapters that follow. However, the reader who looks for a single sustained thesis and a linear progression of thought in these chapters will probably be disappointed, for they do not so much proceed from starting point to conclusion as they, rather, circle again and again around the central tension between agape and philia and explore that tension from various angles. The central element in this tension, as I perceive it, is the preferential character of friendship. The opening chapter deals with that problem directly, and—after chapters discussing the related problems of reciprocity and fidelity in friendship—I return to the problem of preference and particularity in considering politics and vocation, both spheres which can lay claim to more universality than can friendship.

It should be clear even from this brief description that this is not a "how to" book designed to help anyone gain friends or keep them. On that topic I would scarcely consider myself a reliable guide. Nor are these chapters a discussion of the shape friendship has taken at different periods of Western history, though I hope they do not unduly distort what historians have discovered. Nor are they, even, attempts to display in full-blown form any of the classical theories of friendship, though considerable attention is paid to thinkers such as Plato, Aristotle, Cicero, and Augustine. Instead, this is intended as a study in theological ethics. I bring to the topic of friendship my own theologically shaped notion of what is important and use it to focus my discussion in ways which, I hope, prove illuminating. Others, perhaps, would take as their chief concern some different aspect of friendship; the Christian ethicist, it seems to me, can scarcely avoid concerning himself with problems of preference, reciprocity, and fidelity. In short, this is to some extent a case study in what used to be called the relation of nature and grace. And if the discerning reader perceives in my obvious unwillingness to transcend some tensions a certain residual Lutheranism, I hope the matter of the discussion will also bear witness to a growing appreciation of Catholicism.

I seek not to praise agape at the expense of philia but to probe their interrelationships. Indeed, a Christian ethic which could really do no more than uproot a natural bond of such fundamental human significance as friendship would be for me—in the strictest sense of the word—incredible. In fact, insofar as there is any polemical urge in these chapters, it is the urge to make place within Christian ethics—even honored place—for a particular bond such as philia. But when all that is said and done, it is still true that "when friendships were the noblest things in the world, charity was little." That datum suggests something important, even in certain ways authoritative, which the Christian ethicist must heed.

1. Friendship as a Preferential Love

> Emma perceived that her taste was not the only taste
> on which Mr. Weston depended, and felt that to be the
> favourite and intimate of a man who has so many inti-
> mates and confidants was not the very first distinction
> in the scale of vanity. She liked his open manners, but a
> little less of open-heartedness would have made him a
> higher character. General benevolence, but not general
> friendship, made a man what he ought to be.
>
> Jane Austen, *Emma*

In our world, where "friend" often means little more
than "acquaintance," where "friend" must be preceded
by various modifiers (business friend, bridge friend), we
may almost forget that the deep intimacy of friendship
at its best involves preference. Western thought about
friendship has grounded that particularity of preference
sometimes in an affective attachment to the friend,
sometimes in a quite impersonal choice of the friend;
but in either case it has been clear that the bond of
friendship, creating "one soul in bodies twain," is a
bond which can be shared with only a few (possibly
even, as Montaigne thought, only one).

Others are excluded. Perhaps it is only when we put
the point this way—a way which offends not so much
our egalitarian theories as our belief that *we* ought
never be treated as outsiders—that the element of
preference which attaches itself to friendship becomes

questionable. Such questioning may be new for us, but it is not new for Western thought. When the streams of classical thought about friendship and the Christian teaching of agape flow together, the ideal of particular friendship becomes haunted by the requirement of universal love. If Christian love means (as Kierkegaard put it) "not to make distinctions" in love, can one be a friend only with a bad conscience?[1] It is a serious question—serious for theological ethics, serious for those who wish to know how we ought to live. Friendship raises for us the problem of preference in love. In his *Life of Johnson* Boswell recounts a conversation of Dr. Johnson with, among others, a Mrs. Knowles. She suggests that friendship is a Christian virtue, opposing thereby a contrary view in a recently published book by Soame Jenyns. Dr. Johnson responds:

> Why, Madam, strictly speaking he is right. All friendship is preferring the interest of a friend, to the neglect, or, perhaps, against the interest of others; so that an old Greek said, "He that has *friends* has *no friend*." Now Christianity recommends universal benevolence, to consider all men as our brethren; which is contrary to the virtue of friendship, as described by the ancient philosphers.

Mrs. Knowles responds by citing the Bible passage requiring that we do good to all but *especially* to those of the household of faith. Johnson replies that "the household of faith is wide enough." Mrs. Knowles responds yet once more, pointing out that though Jesus had twelve apostles we are told that there was one whom he loved.

> JOHNSON (with eyes sparkling benignantly). "Very well, indeed, Madam. You have said very well."
> BOSWELL. "A fine application. Pray, Sir, had you ever thought of it?"
> JOHNSON. "I had not, Sir."

Whether the issue can be quite so easily resolved, we may perhaps doubt. Indeed, we shall return later to consider whether an important distinction may not be buried in what Dr. Johnson equates: *neglecting* the interests of others in order to prefer those of a friend, and *acting against* the interests of others in order to prefer those of a friend. But Dr. Johnson is not mistaken in suggesting that philia, as the ancients experienced it, and agape, as Christians articulated it, may seem incompatible. In order to think about friendship as a preferential love, therefore, we do well to begin with classical thought.

I

It would be false to say that the entire history of Western thought about friendship is a series of footnotes to Plato, but if we said "to Plato and Aristotle," we would begin to approach an important truth: that, if we first bracket from our attention the special questions and problems which Christian belief raises, Plato and Aristotle offer us representative expressions of what may be the two most important competing theories of friendship.[2] For Plato, friendship is a universal love which grows out of more particular, affective attachments. For Aristotle (and for the majority of classical thinkers who, on this point, follow him rather than Plato) it is a narrowing down of the many toward whom we have good will to a few friends whom we especially choose. Plato's theory begins with a particular attachment, which then grows toward a more universal love. Aristotle's moves in precisely the opposite direction. Plato grounds friendship in sentiment; Aristotle in choice.

One of Plato's short Socratic dialogues, the *Lysis*, is devoted to the topic of friendship. If, however, one wants the developed Platonic understanding of philia it is necessary to turn to the *Phaedrus* and the *Sympo-*

sium. We will concentrate here on the former of these. The *Phaedrus* is in many ways a baffling dialogue.[3] Its first half consists of three speeches about love—the first, a speech of Lysias which is read to Socrates by Phaedrus; the second, a speech which Socrates gives in response to the first, but which Socrates himself then immediately disavows; the third, another speech by Socrates, this one asserting a viewpoint precisely contrary to that of the speech he had given but disavowed. The second half of the dialogue consists in puzzling discussions of questions of rhetoric: whether the written word is preferable to the spoken, what constitutes a beautiful speech, and so forth. We will bypass the difficult question of the relation between the halves of the dialogue in order to concentrate on what is said about love in the speeches which constitute the first half.

Socrates and Phaedrus meet on a street in Athens as Phaedrus is preparing to go for a walk outside the walls and rehearse a speech he has heard given by Lysias, a Sophist who writes speeches for others. Phaedrus is much taken by this speech and assumes that Socrates will be as well, so Socrates easily persuades Phaedrus to read the speech for him. Lysias has written the speech for a man who seeks the favors of a handsome young boy but who does not love the boy.[4] Hence, the speech is an attempt to persuade the boy that he would do better to give his favors to one who seeks only pleasure without emotional attachment. In that way he will get pleasure without the accompanying complications which love brings. The man seeks, in Josef Pieper's words, "gratification without eros." Plato will, through the mouth of Socrates in the third speech, advocate the opposite: "eros without gratification."

When the speech has been read, Socrates tells Phaedrus, much to the latter's disappointment, that as a piece of rhetoric the speech is inferior. Under prodding from Phaedrus, he agrees to try to offer another and better speech on the same topic. He constructs a speech to be spoken by one who really loves a boy but who persuades the boy that he does not love him (and, hence, the speaker is one who from the outset announces an intention to deceive). This lover pretending to be a nonlover offers the boy a speech in defense of Lysias's point: that it is better to gratify appetite without the complications which love brings. The argument of Socrates' speech, like that of Lysias, suggests that love is really a sickness. The lover will become possessive; he will try to keep the boy inferior and dependent; he will not be faithful. It is, in fact, a rather persuasive case that Socrates offers, clearly illuminating some of the dangers to which human preferential loves are subject. Whatever its virtues, however, Socrates suddenly breaks off the speech, tells Phaedrus that it has been blasphemous, and claims that before leaving he must give another speech which will recognize the divinity of love and thereby atone for his impiety.

This he does. Socrates' speech in defense of love is vintage Plato, incorporating discussion of the nature of the soul and striking mythical imagery. The essential point of this speech is, however, the simple claim that eros—a preferential love—is of divine origin. In eros the lover is moved by something which goes beyond appetite, beyond even the affective atttachment of eros itself. To make the point Socrates offers the famous image of the soul as a team of winged horses driven by a charioteer. One horse is noble and well-behaved; the other hard to control and unruly. When the soul loses its wings, it can no longer soar on high and must instead fall down into the realm of finitude where it is joined with a body to form a living and mortal human being.

Yet, the soul longs to return on high from whence it came. And the way back is possible not because of reason but because of love. The soul's wings must begin to grow once again. This happens "when a man sees beauty in this world and has a remembrance of true beauty"

(249d). The vision of beauty is a call, but the soul cannot easily or quickly return to gaze on beauty itself. Instead, one must learn gradually, by encounters with beautiful things and beautiful persons, to love beauty. Eros is of divine origin precisely because even in all its earthly manifestations it constitutes a call from what is beyond the finite realm. Thus, when the lover looks upon a beautiful face or form "a shudder runs through him and something of the old awe steals over him" (251a).

The beloved is a sign and a call, but the message may be missed and the call misunderstood. In the moment when the soul is caught by that vision of beauty, the conflict within the soul—between the two steeds—may become evident. "The obedient horse, then as always constrained by decorum, controls itself and does not leap upon the beloved. The other, however, no longer pays any attention to the driver's spur or whip, but leaps wildly forward, . . . trying to force them to approach the beloved and propose the pleasures of love" (254a). The unruly steed can be disciplined and controlled only over a period of time. If this is achieved, what began in eros will end in philia. Eros without gratification means for the lovers a shared life in the pursuit of wisdom. When eros is sublimated, the lovers are able to recognize its character as sign and call and enabled to move beyond it toward that to which it points. In this way eros leads to philosophy; lover and beloved now share in the love of wisdom. Indeed, friendship at its best consists in such a shared love of wisdom, and for Plato philia is the end result of sublimated eros. Friendship becomes thereby at least implicitly universal: open to all who discipline the appetites, recognize the call of eros for what it is, and share in the love of wisdom. Such a love is not exclusive but is potentially universal in scope. The preferential attachment of eros gives way to and is transcended by the universally shared love of wisdom in which true friendship is found.

This is not only a magnificent vision; it is, in addition, a perspective from which particular, preferential loves and a universally shared love may seem to be reconcilable. The former is the means to the latter— possibly the only means. For the Platonist these particular loves must ultimately be sublimated and transcended, but they cannot be simply rejected. Preferential love is not the end toward which one moves, but it is a means to that end. Yet, even to put the matter this way is to raise the crucial problem not only for Plato's view of friendship but for any view which attempts to overcome particular preference in the name of more universal other-regarding love. Particular attachments are here interpreted simply as a means to an end. In that end lies their whole meaning and purpose.

Plato's view seems to suggest that it is not the friend but the form of beauty which inheres in the friend that is loved. And in that case, the friend would seem to be interchangeable with anyone else in whom beauty appears, for it is the same form which appears in many persons. But then has not the friend actually disappeared? To purchase universal love one has paid a high price indeed: the loss of all particular attachments. This becomes quite clear in the famous ascent passage in the *Symposium* (210-212b). One moves from love for the physical beauty of a particular person, to love for the beauty of several, to love for all who share the character of being beautiful, to love of the beautiful wherever it appears, to philosophy (shared love of wisdom), to the Beautiful itself. And Diotima explains to Socrates why the lover ought not attach himself to just one beautiful body:

> he must remark how the beauty attached to this or that
> body is cognate to that which is attached to any other,
> and that if he means to ensue beauty in form, it is gross
> folly not to regard as one and the same the beauty belong-
> ing to all; and so, having grasped this truth, he must make

himself a lover of all beautiful bodies, and slacken the stress of his feeling for one by contemning it and counting it a trifle. (210b)[5]

To "count as a trifle" one's attachment to a friend, however, can scarcely do justice to the significance of the love of friendship in our lives. Perhaps Aristotle, whose feet always seem a bit more firmly planted on the ground, can do better.

"No one," writes Aristotle in his *Nicomachean Ethics*, "would choose to live without friends, even if he had all other goods" (VIII, 1).[6] For Aristotle, philia can often be a term having a scope much wider than we would ordinarily give it. Any bond that gives people something in common and holds them together he can term philia. Hence, the notion of "civic friendship," a bond which holds the members of a political community together, makes perfect sense to Aristotle, though it plays little part in our lives today. Furthermore, Aristotle provides several different classifications of friendship— one based on what it is that we love in the friend, another based on whether or not the partners in friendship are equal or unequal. Friends can be loved, Aristotle thinks, because they are useful, or because they are pleasant, or because they are good.[7] The highest form of friendship arises at the intersection of the two classifications: when those who are equal choose one another as friends, not merely for the sake of pleasure or advantage, but because of the other's character.

Aristotle clearly thinks that friendship of this highest sort is preferential and particular. It may be possible to please many people on the basis of the advantage or pleasure one brings them, but "to be friends with many people, in the sense of perfect friendship, is impossible" (VIII, 6). Indeed, for Aristotle philia is in some ways the narrowing down of a more universally other-regarding disposition, good will (*eunoia*). He notes that though friendship and good will may appear similar, they are

not the same. It is possible to have good will toward
those whom we do not really know and who could, therefore, not reciprocate our good will. Hence, Aristotle
characterizes good will as "the beginning of friendship"
or even as friendship in an extended but "inactive"
sense (IX, 5). It is impossible for friendship to spring up
if this more generalized good will is not first present,
but the mere presence of good will does not guarantee
that the particular relation of friendship will in fact
arise. That more narrow relationship requires reciprocity and active assistance, and these will arise only if
each finds the character of the other to be admirable
and choiceworthy.

   That such a genuine friendship must be preferential
Aristotle never doubts, and he helps us see what such a
special bond of attachment must involve. To be a friend
is to incur obligation. Aristotle writes that

> the gravity of an unjust act increases in proportion as the
> person to whom it is done is a closer friend. It is, for ex-
> ample, more shocking to defraud a bosom companion of
> money than a fellow citizen, to refuse help to a brother
> than to refuse it to a stranger, or to strike one's father
> than to strike any other person. It is natural that the
> element of justice increases with [the closeness of] the
> friendship. . . . (VIII, 9)

There is something eminently reasonable about such a
viewpoint. The stranger comes with no set of expectations or loyalties toward us. With the friend, however,
our previous pattern of behavior has fashioned a relationship in which the friend has reason to anticipate
certain treatment from us. By giving ourselves to the
friend in this special bond of attachment we create in
him a set of needs, expectations, and loyalties. Therefore, the wrong we do him takes on not only the character of injustice but of betrayal, even treason.[8] We can
understand why Aristotle would say that the gravity of
the offense increases when it is done to a friend.

This *is* eminently reasonable. But is it satisfactory? If, as Dr. Johnson remarked to Mrs. Knowles, "Christianity recommends universal benevolence, to consider all men as our brethren," we may be moved to wonder. There is something very natural about the attitude Aristotle expresses; yet, the simple force of Jesus' story of the Good Samaritan calls that "naturalness" and "reasonableness" into question. Part of the force of Jesus' story lies in the fact that it should be a Samaritan who stops to help the man beaten and lying by the side of the road. These men are, in the cultural circumstances of their day, "strangers" to each other. There can be no thought of any prior set of expectations or loyalties, no relationship which would have created any special obligations. Yet, the suggestion of the story seems to be that all members of the human community have been given over into each other's care, not simply those who have given themselves in special bonds such as friendship. The implicit point seems to be that the stranger, just as much as the friend, has a claim upon us for all the care and consideration we can muster and that to fail here would be not only an injustice but also a betrayal of our common humanity.

Aristotle's view is not entirely without safeguards. He recognizes, for example, that one is not entitled to give unlimited consideration to one's friend(s). We will have obligations not only to our friends but to our parents, our benefactors, and so forth. We must "render what is appropriate and fitting to each" (IX, 2). Aristotle clearly thinks, for instance, that we would be mistaken to lavish all our favors upon our friends and show no gratitude to others who have helped us. Thus, the preference we may show those bound to us by friendship is limited by the preference we ought to show those bound to us in other ways. One special relation limits another, and, indeed, there can be little doubt that much of the moral life involves various competing obligations of this sort. Furthermore, we ought not forget the sense in which philia for Aristotle is also a very generalized bond for a whole society. He is perhaps the last Greek thinker to try to hold particularity and (some) universality together in his understanding of friendship.[9] On the one hand, philia is clearly a particular bond possible only for those of a certain character. On the other, anyone who has such character will, Aristotle thinks, approach all fellow-citizens as having the potential to become close friends. Still it is hard to see this as anything more than the generalized good will which is, at best, "inactive" friendship.

Even when we have made these qualifications there remains in Aristotle's concept of friendship a kind of contented exclusivity which may trouble us. One feels the need for a little more of that openness which Plato's view of friendship as transcended eros has. That view runs the danger, as we saw, of losing particular attachment entirely in devotion to what is universal. But it at least does lift the friends out of their egocentricity. It has a virtue which Aristotle's description of friendship lacks: the recognition that attachment to our friends cannot bear the weight Aristotle places upon it. Perhaps—so at least Plato's theory would suggest—the love of friendship is safe only when it is understood to lead beyond itself, only when it is believed to be an image of and preparation for some greater love in a greater and more universal community. For the development of such a view we turn to St. Augustine.

There are references to friendship scattered in many places throughout Augustine's writings; one of the most famous and instructive, however, is his discussion of the death of a friend in his *Confessions* (IV, 4-12). Reflection on the death of his friend leads Augustine to consider the nature of attachment to a friend and the relation of this love to love of God. Platonist that he always remained, Augustine believes that the love of friendship is a sign and a call intended to draw the friends on toward love of God.

If bodies please you, praise God for them and turn your love back from them to their maker, lest you should displease Him in being pleased by them. If souls please you, love them in God, because by themselves they are subject to change, but in Him they are established firm; without Him they would pass away and be no more. So you must love them in Him. . . . For He did not make things and then go away; things are from Him and also in Him. (IV, 12)[10]

That is the lesson Augustine draws from consideration of his own grief at the death of his friend. He concludes, not that he had been mistaken to attach himself to the friend, but that he had mistaken a sign and a call for a resting place. He had, he says, loved the friend "as if he were an immortal" (IV, 8). One ought rather to praise God for beauties such as the love of a friend without resting the whole weight of the heart's longing in them. "For these things go along their path toward nonexistence, and they tear and wound the soul with terrible longings, since the soul itself desires to be and to find rest in what it loves" (IV, 10).

For Augustine, as for Plato, attachment to the friend must be transformed. The friend is to be loved in God. "Augustine gives the widest possible scope to friendships. He is referring, of course, to fraternal charity, and yet . . . his ideal was to have the unity which is an integral part of individual friendship reign among all men in fraternal charity."[11] The highest form of friendship, intimated by our particular friendships, is that which joins all who share the love of God. Thus, particular friendships (philia) are transcended in caritas, God's love which unites those who are his. Yet, caritas itself, though universal in scope, does not lack the intimacy of philia. Hence, there is a kind of double movement in Augustine's thought about friendship. Particular friendships are to school us in love; they are a sign and a call by which God draws us toward a love more universal in scope. Philia is transcended in caritas but not destroyed, for the intensely personal sharing which friendship involves is added to charity as its internal fruition.

That picture of friendship transformed by universal charity is, of course, a picture of heaven. There, perhaps, preferential philia may safely be added to universal caritas. The justification for preference in this life, however, must for Augustine lie largely in friendship's function as a school of virtue. Since this is the case, two questions arise: (1) Does Augustine, like Plato, finally purchase universal love at the cost (at least in this life) of all particular attachments? And (2) once we have come to see the goal toward which philia calls us, how can we justify continuing to enjoy our preferential loves rather than pressing as best we can toward that goal of universal love even in this life? The answers to these questions are interrelated.

If love for the friend is only a school to teach us a love far more universal in scope, will not anyone do as a friend? Does not that very conception of friendship eliminate, in fact, the preference which is an integral, necessary, and valued aspect of friendship in our experience? It does not for Augustine, for the quite simple reason that he has Christianized his Platonism. There can be, Augustine writes, "no true friendship unless those who cling to each other are welded together by you in that love which is spread throughout our hearts by the holy spirit which is given to us" (IV, 4). The friend is God's gift. In loving the friend as a sign of and call from God himself, in referring the friend back to God, as Augustine says, and loving the particular friend in God, we do not lose the friend or make the friend interchangeable with anyone else. In referring back to God the friend whom God gives, we continually receive the friend back from God. The friend is loved properly—"in God"—and understood as God's gift, yet still truly loved in God. The God toward whom the friend is meant to lead us is the God who gives the friend.

In his treatise *On Christian Doctrine* (I, xxviii) Augustine offers an intriguing suggestion for relating preferential loves to the universal love of charity.

All men are to be loved equally. But since you cannot do good to all, you are to pay special regard to those who, by the accidents of time, or place, or circumstance, are brought into closer connection with you. For, suppose that you had a great deal of some commodity, and felt bound to give it away to somebody who had none, and that it could not be given to more than one person; if two persons presented themselves, neither of whom had either from need or relationship a greater claim upon you than the other, you could do nothing fairer than choose by lot to which you would give what could not be given to both. Just so among men, since you cannot consult for the good of them all, you must take the matter as decided for you by a sort of lot, according as each man happens for the time being to be more closely connected with you.[12]

The notion of a "divine lottery" by which we are joined to others in particular ties may seem to us rather quaint; yet there is a good bit of wisdom hidden in it. Preferential loves inevitably involve "time, or place, or circumstance." And, from the perspective of universal love there can be no doubt that these are what Augustine calls them: accidents. From the perspective of the eternal, it is hard to see why such accidents could be decisive, why they should justify preference in love. Augustine, however, does not conclude from this that preference in love is illegitimate. Instead, he suggests that within the finite, historical realm these "accidents" are God's doing. We cannot in this finite life "consult for the good of them all," nor achieve a love which is truly universal. The particular loves are the means God uses to lead his creatures toward the universal love of caritas, but they are still the means God has chosen.

The lottery is a divine lottery. And there is something very instructive in coming to see that the particular bonds of time, place, and circumstance are accidents in one sense but not in another. They are accidents in that, from the perspective of the goal of universal love, they can be of no ultimate importance. Thus, we are not to think that there really is something just a little special about our particular group of friends—that, though we might not put it quite this way in public, there are many people who would not be worthy of entering our circle of friends. No, such thoughts are to be banished by the recognition that these preferential loves are the result of the accidents of time, place, and circumstance. They are merely the school in which we learn what it would be like to love anyone, in which we become open and ready to receive others. Yet, of course, they are not accidents in another sense; they are the gift of God, and it is quite right that we should delight in the friends given us. The special bond of friendship is, for one who thinks like Augustine, part of the Creator's ordering of human life. In that sense it is no accident—while it remains true that there is no reason *other than* the Creator's gift and ordering why we should be bound to these particular persons rather than to others. Our friends are not really people of more worth; that cannot be the reason they are special. In learning to care for them we may learn what it would mean to care for any human being. We may learn, that is, a love which is implicitly universal.

Seeing this, we can understand why, within this life, we cannot leap over these preferential loves to a love which is truly universal in scope. "The friend is not lost in the Absolute, nor left behind as a step in the ascent, but is a permanent revelation of God, a necessary complement to the soul in its movement to God."[13] The pilgrimage toward God is limited by the constraints of time and place, constraints which bind us to some in special relations of love. These special bonds can never fully satisfy the longing of the heart for God, for they remain partial goods which cannot be shared with all. It is, therefore, in their very nature to be preparatory for the city of God's love which will exist beyond the limits of time and place. Augustine draws a comparison with our powers of speech and understanding. For creatures such as we are, the pleasure of "perceiving the entirety of things" is not a possibility. We can only understand words (or, perhaps, even syllables) as they come to us singly and as we comprehend them *seriatim*. We want the whole sentence; we get only words, each of which passes away before we get the next (IV, 11). Existence in time makes necessary particular attachments rather than a bond of universal love. Even so, however, the friend must always be referred back to God and loved in God. Only then do we love as creatures ought. Only then is the friend loved as what he truly is — a creature.

Elements of each of the chief classical views of friendship are taken up and transformed in Augustine's discussion. The recognition that friendship must necessarily be particular and preferential, that, as Aristotle said (IX, 10), "it is quite obvious that it is impossible to live together with many people and divide oneself up among them" — all that finds an important place in Augustine's description of friendship. At the same time, however, these particular friendships are placed in a larger context, seen as a call toward and preparation for a love more universal in scope. And both aspects are incorporated into Augustine's theological vision. Particular friendships are justified because, in the simplest sense, God gives them to those whom he has created to live within the constraints of finitude. Particular friendships are qualified because this same God intends that they should lead us toward the love of God in which all the redeemed will share and be a school in which that love is learned. Hence, Augustine's understanding of friendship is transformed when it is placed within his vision of human life as pilgrimage. One is sustained by

the vision of universal love toward which one is drawn,
but the way to that goal leads through particular bonds
of affection and attachment. For, as Augustine himself
put it, "it is one thing to see from a mountaintop in the
forests the land of peace in the distance . . . and it is
another. thing to hold to the way that leads there"
(VII, 21).

II

In St. Augustine we find a Christian thinker who,
without ignoring the differences between friendship and
Christian love, manages to fashion a positive connection
between them. It is, of course, his conception of Christian love as caritas—a love which draws the self toward
God and loves the friend in God—which enables him to
do this. The positive connection is fashioned by beginning with the love that is particular and preferential,
recognizing its partial character, and permitting it then
to function as a sign of and call toward a love more
universal in scope.

Such a view, however, has not seemed adequate to
all Christian thinkers, some of whom have thought that
the direction of movement ought to be the reverse of
what it is in Augustine. They have thought that it was
incumbent upon Christians to begin with universal
love—true charity—and justify particular loves, if at
all, on the basis of Christian love in the fullest sense.[14]
Where Augustine begins with the natural, earthly love
and seeks to "build up" from it to love of God and the
friend in God, others have preferred to begin with a
love universal in scope (similar to Aristotle's good will)
and "build down" to particular attachments as specifi-
cations of universal love.

Jonathan Edwards, for example, describing true
virtue in the rather abstract language of "benevolence
to being in general," explains that this need not require
that "being in general" be the "direct and immediate

object of every virtuous act," but that "the nature of
true virtue consists in a disposition to benevolence
towards being in general; though from such a disposition may arise exercises of love to particular beings, as
objects are presented and occasions arise."[15] Exactly
how such particular exercises of love arise from a disposition of benevolence toward being in general may not
be immediately clear, but the basic thrust of Edwards's
position and the sense in which its direction of movement is opposite to that of Augustine ought to be evident. To be sure, some part of the difference in their
views lies in differing assessments of the dynamic power
of particular loves such as friendship. Edwards, for
example, views "particular instincts of nature" as de-
fective because they are essentially "private." By this
he means that "they do not arise from any temper of
benevolence to being in general, nor have they a tendency to such effect in their operation."[16] This criticism
reveals an understanding of particular loves quite
different from that of St. Augustine. It is unlikely that
Augustine would acquiesce in either of these explanations of the "private" character of special bonds of love.
He might grant that a love like friendship does not
"arise from any temper of benevolence to being in
general"; however, he might also contend that in loving
the friend we experience (as Plato suggested) a "shudder" before beauty and that when "something of the old
awe steals over" us we are in fact seeking an object of
love more universal and satisfying than the friend alone.
Certainly, Augustine would not acquiesce in Edwards's
claim that particular loves have in their operation no
"tendency" toward benevolence toward being in general.
Quite the contrary—for Augustine a particular love
such as friendship is characterized by a kind of dynamic
power which is, in fact, the dynamism of love. Josef
Pieper reminds us of Dante's words when Beatrice
appeared—"no foe existed for me any more"—and
comments: "If we look to the well-documented experi-

ence of great lovers we learn that precisely this intensity of love turned toward a single partner seems to place the lover at a vantage point from which he realises for the first time the goodness and lovableness of all people, in fact of all living beings."[17] That is Augustine's dynamism of love: any particular love, taken seriously, will draw us beyond its own particularity toward the One who is love itself. It is also true, of course, that sinful human nature will regularly resist this dynamic pull which natural love exhibits. Natural, preferential love can be not only a school of virtue but a school of vice, as a stanza of George Herbert's "The Sacrifice" nicely suggests:

> They binde, and leade me unto *Herod:* he
> Sends me to *Pilate*. This makes them agree;
> But yet their friendship is my enmitie:
> Was ever grief like mine?

That it is possible to stop short of the final resting place in God, Augustine does not of course deny. Indeed, his entire understanding of inordinate love is a description of such a premature halt, a refusal to follow the dynamic movement of love to the goal toward which it leads. What Augustine does deny, however, is that the longing of the heart can be truly satisfied by any such premature halt, by any object of love short of God himself. Part of the difference between Edwards and Augustine lies, therefore, in differing assessments of the dynamic force of the particular loves. Because Augustine believes that particular attachments will (by God's gracious ordination) lead on toward their appointed goal, he is willing to see them as a necessary starting point even if not the end of one's pilgrimage. Edwards, by contrast, cannot regard any bond of love as virtuous which is not a narrowing and specifying of universal and general benevolence.

If we ask how a particular bond such as friendship may arise from a love universal in scope, Edwards does not offer much help. But Jeremy Taylor exemplifies such an attempt—the effort to justify particular loves on the basis of universal charity. The Anglican divine begins his "Discourse on the Nature and Offices of Friendship"[18] by noting candidly that "the word 'friendship' in the sense we commonly mean by it, is not so much as named in the New Testament, and our religion takes no notice of it" (p. 71). If, however, friendship means the "greatest love and the greatest usefulness, and the most open communication"—then, he writes, this affection has been newly christened by Christianity and called "charity" (p. 72). Furthermore, Taylor is quite aware of the remarkable historical changes worked by this christening. "Christian charity is friendship to all the world; and when friendships were the noblest things in the world, charity was little" (p. 72). He is quite candid in recognizing that the classical ideal of friendship appears to clash with the highest love known to Christians. Friendship as it was understood in the classical world and as we ourselves still commonly think of it—preferential and exclusive—has been displaced by that neighbor-love which is, at least potentially, "friendship to all the world." Thus, the preference so deeply rooted in friendship gives way to a nonpreferential and nonexclusive love. Taylor expresses the point in a fine phrase, which has roots in English historical experience. "When men contract friendships," he writes, "they enclose the commons; and what nature intended should be every man's, we make proper to two or three" (p. 72). Christianity, on the other hand, means an extension of the affections. When this faith entered the world "it was declared that our friendships were to be as universal as our conversation; that is, actual to all with whom we converse, and potentially extended unto those with whom we did not" (p. 73).

The reader of these opening paragraphs of Taylor's *Discourse* may therefore be somewhat surprised to find that the bulk of the treatise consists of an attempt to justify for Christians "a dear and perfect friendship" which is preferential and exclusive. The very labor he bestows on this effort is testimony to the importance such special bonds have for human life—even, one might say, testimony to the wound inflicted on our nature by any doctrine requiring "friendship to all the world." We give the ancients their due only when we recognize how quickly universal love can become an inhumane requirement rather than an inspiring ideal.

Part of Taylor's case justifying particular friendships involves language similar to that of Augustine, no doubt because Augustine had bequeathed his vision to Christendom. Our preferential loves are still "imperfect," Taylor writes, and they are "but the beginnings of a celestial friendship, by which we shall love every one as much as they can be loved" (p. 73). He can even use the language of "accidents"—suggesting that differentiation comes into our "friendship to all the world" only because of the accidents of time and place—recalling thereby Augustine's divine lottery. This language leads to his central argument, that grounded in the constraints of finitude.

Various people are "near" to me, Taylor writes. Some are near by relation, some may have done me benefit, some may literally pass by me, some I may have a particular fancy for—in all these ways and many others special bonds can arise. The effect of this is that limits enter into universal friendship. Our general benevolence "must be limited, because we are so" (p. 74). And here Taylor makes an important distinction. Considerations of finitude do not mean that "friendship to all the world" is entirely forgotten. No, it still has its role to play. For in certain matters "we stand next to immensity and infinity" (p. 74). That is, we have some goods which can be stretched almost indefinitely—most particularly, our prayers and our good wishes. Even in a finite world, universal love must express itself in these ways. But where such universal regard "is impossible, it cannot be necessary" (p. 75). Thus Taylor concludes, a bit complacently perhaps, that "there are more reasons to love some than others; and if I must love because there is reason I should, then I must love more where there is more reason" (p. 75). "Friendship to all the world" has now been restricted in scope in a way that admits of succinct description: "men can pray for one another, and abstain from doing injuries to all the world, and be desirous to do all mankind good, and love all men" (p. 75). It has become an essentially negative principle —do no harm—retaining its overtones of active concern for all only in the fact that we are enjoined to wish well to all and pray for all.

I do not mean to suggest that prayer for and good will toward all human beings are unimportant; indeed, perhaps we do not appreciate how seriously one like Jeremy Taylor took such considerations. Still, one wonders whether he has not in fact given us something that looks remarkably like what Aristotle gave us: certain special bonds of attachment arising from a more all-encompassing good will which deserves to be called no more than Aristotle called it—"inactive friendship." Taylor himself writes that friendship is "charity that is fitted for society" (p. 81). Quite possibly true, but hardly a principle calculated to transform a world built around preferential loves—which is how Taylor had described charity.

At any rate, we may doubt whether Taylor has demonstrated how particular friendships as we experience them could actually be justified within a charity which is "friendship to all the world"—even when that charity is differentiated by the constraints of finitude. What he really seems to give us is a Christianity teaching a higher nonpreferential love and *in addition* praising a preferential love such as friendship. And it may be true, as Kierkegaard wrote, that "it is an impossibility to love according to both explanations simultaneously."[19] Kierkegaard provides an apt illustration explaining why this is the case. To find a friend is no easy task. It requires consideration of the other's character, his interests, his abilities—literally, almost everything that makes the friend the particular person he is. On the other hand, "there is in the whole world not a single person who can be recognised with such ease and certainty as one's neighbour. You can never confuse him with anyone else, for indeed all men are your neighbour."[20] What such neighbor-love may mean for the preferential love of friendship becomes quite clear when Kierkegaard draws the conclusion: "If you save a man's life in the dark, supposing him to be your friend, but he is your neighbour, this again is no mistake."[21] It is no mistake because when we are speaking of neighbor-love, of "friendship to all the world," it really makes no difference.[22]

But—and here Taylor's valiant attempt to ground friendship in charity fails—friendships are built on differences. It is these differences which lead us to prefer the friend. Our finite condition may explain why we cannot love everyone; it will give no justification for preferential (as opposed to random) choice of those whom we do love. Friendship cannot, it seems, be accounted for and built into charity simply because of the constraints of finitude. A particular love like friendship has its own "urgencies" which cannot be explained as arising from universal charity plus finitude.[23] I do not necessarily become friends with the first person who happens along. Age and intellectual endowments will play their part; more important still will be shared interests and values; perhaps more important still, though harder to define, will be some judgment about the total character of the other person. The more think of friendship as we actually experience it, the more it begins to sound like a love quite different from Christian love, a love which does indeed "enclose the commons." If we are to praise it, we may have to do so not because it arises as a species of universal love but because it has its own validity *in addition* to "friendship to all the world."

One way to do this is to affirm the distinction toward which Jeremy Taylor was inexorably driven and which Dr. Johnson made in his response to Mrs. Knowles: the distinction between neglecting the interests of some people in order to care for others and intentionally acting against the well-being of some in order to bring aid to others. To abstain from doing injury and injustice to all may be a task more possible than genuine "friendship to all the world." It may also be a task more appropriate to those who are creatures. We may put the point more strongly by saying that to make universal love the one fundamental principle of morality and to attempt to derive particular attachments and obligations from it may fail to recognize that, unlike God, we cannot and ought not make "general well-being" the focus of our concern. In a typically dense but important paragraph, Joseph Butler makes precisely this point.

The fact then appears to be, that we are constituted so as to condemn falsehood, unprovoked violence, injustice, and to approve of benevolence to some preferably to others abstracted from all consideration, which conduct is likely to produce an overbalance of happiness or misery; and therefore, *were the Author of Nature to propose nothing to Himself as an end but the production of happiness, were His moral character merely that of benevolence; yet ours is not so.* Upon that supposition indeed the only reason of His giving us the above mentioned approbation of benevolence to some persons rather than others, and disapprobation of falsehood, unprovoked violence and injustice, must be that He foresaw this constitution of our nature would produce more happiness than forming us with a temper of mere general benevolence. But still, since this is our constitution, falsehood, violence, injustice, must be vice in us, and benevolence to some preferably to others, virtue, abstracted from all consideration of the overbalance of evil or good which they may appear likely to produce.[24]

That is to say, "friendship to all the world" is a mistaken ideal to apply to those who are creatures, not Creator. It leads (as with Taylor and Edwards) to grudging concessions made to the constraints of time, space, and particular bonds of affection rather than glad affirmation of these as essential for human existence. At the same time, one can say this without denying that the human community—and our moral obligations—extend beyond the limited sphere of our preferential loves. Injustice, falsehood, and violence are, as Butler put it, "vice in us" and cannot be transformed into virtue merely by being done in the service of friendship.

An adequate moral theory must recognize that there are various goods in and for human life, that none of us can realize all these goods in our own life, and that, therefore, any choices to affirm and cultivate certain goods must mean the neglect of others.[25] Really to devote oneself to relief of pain and suffering in the world may, for example, leave little time for the cultivation of deep personal friendships. And the reverse may also be true. If a view like Butler's is correct, we must say that either of these options is choiceworthy. What is not to be countenanced, however, is a choice to realize one such good by any means which intentionally brings harm to others. To damage the reputation of a third party in order to enhance the cause of a friend is to do active harm to a "neighbor," not merely to neglect one good in order to foster another. Our choice of friends and our attachment to them may, therefore, be exclusive without being exclusivistic. To say that we are friends with only a few, that we devote a relatively large portion of our energy and resources to their well-being, is only to describe a relation fundamental to human life which may be chosen to the neglect of certain other goods which might otherwise have been realized. However, it is morally quite different to take pleasure in the fact that some are excluded from our friendship, to refuse to hold that friendship open to newcomers who may share our interests and values—in short, to choose a friendship which is exclusive by design rather than by circumstance. To devote time, energy, and concern to one's friends is not active concern for all human beings, but it can be chosen and done in a way which remains open to all neighbors or in a way which does not. Only the latter is forbidden.

To prefer some to others, but to remain open to those others and refuse to harm them for the sake of those we prefer—this may not be "friendship to all the world," but it can be defended as a legitimate way of incorporating the love of friendship as we actually experience it into a system of Christian belief. As Butler put it,

> The happiness of the world is the concern of Him who is the Lord and Proprietor of it; nor do we know what we are about when we endeavour to promote the good of mankind in any ways but those which He has directed, that is indeed in all ways not contrary to veracity and justice.[26]

Within these limits—limits which will not permit us to conflate, as Dr. Johnson did, neglecting the interests of others for the sake of a friend with preferring the friend's interests against those of others—the love of friendship may be defended. At the same time, however, it is important to add what Augustine seems to have seen far more clearly than Butler: that the dynamic force of love itself will constantly strain against those limits. It is not just a matter of "remaining open" to others while attaching ourselves especially to some. Rather, if I read Augustine correctly, what we can learn from him is that real love for any human being, requiring as it does a disciplining of the selfish impulses, will begin to create in us a new openness toward others. To be sure, we can refuse to learn the lesson love teaches, but our refusal is not to be blamed on preferential love itself. The dynamic power of love, if heeded, will, in Reinhold Niebuhr's words, constantly suggest "purer and broader ideals of brotherhood than any which are realized in any actual community."[27] It will leave little room for the hint of complacency with the restricted character of preferential loves which one can detect not only in Aristotle but in Butler and Taylor as well.

III

The justification of friendship as a particular, preferential love suggested in the preceding sections can be summarized in this way: The particular attachment of friendship need not be grounded in any more universally other-regarding form of love. As the gift of the Creator, it has (for the creature) its own legitimate place in human life. At the same time, the natural love of friendship remains a partial love. It cannot be understood rightly—nor be entirely safe—unless it is seen as intimation of and preparation for a greater love. By the grace of God the natural love of friendship can be taken up and transformed by love for God (Augustine's caritas), and in God it can press toward "friendship to all the world." In this way friendship is charity fitted for society, but the fit is never perfect. The love of friendship continually strains against the limits that would "fit" it into place, since from the perspective of the goal toward which it leads those limits are seen as partial. Furthermore, the claims of friendship can, at best, justify service to the friend the cost of which may be some neglect of others. It cannot justify intentional harm to another for the sake of the friend.

We have there a view which does not attempt to derive friendship from nonpreferential Christian love (which may be impossible) but which does attempt to take seriously the love which is to be shown every neighbor. A natural love like friendship, though not the same as specifically Christian love, manifests something of the fruition love seeks: fellowship with the other. In Daniel Day Williams's words, love is "spirit seeking the enjoyment of freedom in communion with the other."[28]

It may be, though, that this view of love, even when its preferential character is qualified as it is above, does not do full justice to the spirit of Christian love. For there is a type of Christian love—what, to make an overly simple juxtaposition, Protestants have termed agape and contrasted with caritas—which seeks simply to affirm and serve the well-being of the neighbor without any thought of fellowship or communion with the other as the fruition of that service. Such a love can take at least two forms, one "fitted for society," another rather ill-suited to society. It is possible to think of one's vocation as service done in love for the neighbor and to find one's place in a whole system of vocations used by God to care for many neighbors. Such a viewpoint has been characteristically Protestant, and we will return in a later chapter to consider the claims of friendship and the claims of vocation.

Service to the neighbor may also take on a shape very hard to fit into the limits and constraints of society—a love akin to what Daniel Day Williams has called Franciscan love or what Gene Outka has described in discussing love as self-sacrifice.[29] Such a love, because it seeks its own no more than Christ did, breaks through all the normal forms of life in society. Free of all claims to power, privilege, and possession—free even of all desires except the one overmastering desire to follow Christ—this type of Christian lover goes out in search of his neighbor. He seeks no particular goal, not even that of fellowship with the neighbor. He seeks only to make the way of Christ his own and may be quite certain that this way is likely to lead to a cross. This is an agape which cuts through and "transvalues" all the partial loves and attachments in our lives. It serves the neighbor—any neighbor—by refusing to make its own claims or seek fulfillment of its own desires. Reinhold Niebuhr has characterized such a love in this way:

It is impossible to symbolize the divine goodness in history in any other way than by complete powerlessness, or rather by a consistent refusal to use power in the rivalries of history. For there is no self in history or society, no matter how impartial its perspective upon the competitions of life, which can rise to the position of a disinterested participation in those rivalries and competitions. It can symbolize disinterested love only by a refusal to participate in the rivalries.[30]

From the perspective of such love one need not regard friendship as an evil; rather, it is simply one of the goods which must be sacrificed by those who have been grasped by Christ and called to follow him.

We should not underestimate how deeply rooted in Christian thought such heedless neighbor-love is, even though the ideal has perhaps rarely been fully lived. One need think only of Jesus' story of the Good Samaritan to see that such purely disinterested love which breaks through all societal patterns must have serious claims on Christian behavior. "The most characteristic aspect of the Samaritan's behavior is that it is not of this world."[31] He is evidently not journeying to visit a "dear and particular friend" (to use Jeremy Taylor's phrase), since delaying his travel poses no problem. He evidently is bound by no special ties to others—family or friends—who might have a claim on his resources, since he writes a blank check for the innkeeper. His is, indeed, not a love fitted for society; yet, of course, Jesus tells the lawyer to go and do likewise.

Such "Franciscan love" is not merely a supererogatory possibility; neither can it be simply required of all Christians. We must content ourselves with saying— however incomplete and unsatisfying it may seem— that this is one way in which Christian love may take shape in human life, even as the view of love I sketched when drawing on Butler and Augustine is another. A love like that of the Samaritan can, without denigrating the natural love of friendship given us by the Creator, move us to try to live even now as if the process by which the partial, preferential loves are transformed into nonpreferential neighbor-love were completed. That some Christians will feel called to live in this way remains a permanent (and important) possibility. We can object only if it is claimed that this possibility must be required of all—that it is a higher, rather than simply different, form of love—and that all of us must try to live as if the end of history were already fully realized. Against such a claim one would have to place Augustine's image of life as pilgrimage, a journey in which a love like that of friendship has its rightful place. For even if Kierkegaard is correct in saying that "distinction is temporality's confusing element . . . , but neighbour is eternity's mark,"[32] it remains true that temporality is the mark of the creature. To claim that all must strive to transcend that mark would be mistaken—but equally mistaken would be the claim that none should.

2. Friendship as a Reciprocal Love

> We may well wonder whether the general disparagement
> of wanting to be loved may not be a typically modern
> phenomenon, still another form of modern man's claim
> to equality with God.
>
> Josef Pieper, *About Love*

In Plato's *Lysis* there is at one point the following
exchange between Socrates and Menexenus (212a-d):

S: Answer me this. As soon as one man loves another,
which of the two becomes the friend—the lover of the
loved, or the loved of the lover? Or does it make no
difference?

M: None in the world that I can see, he replied.

S: How? said I. Are both friends, if only one loves?

M: I think so, he answered.

S: Indeed! Is it not possible for one who loves, not to be
loved in return by the object of his love?

M: It is.

S: Nay, is it not possible for him even to be hated—treatment, if I mistake not, which lovers frequently fancy
they receive at the hands of their favorites? Though
they love their darlings as dearly as possible, they
often imagine that they are not loved in return, often
that they are even hated. Don't you believe this to
be true?

M: Quite true, he replied.

S: Well, in such a case as this, the one loves, the other
is loved.

M: Just so.

S: Which of the two, then, is the friend of the other—the lover of the loved, whether or no he be loved in return, and even if he be hated, or the loved of the lover? Or is neither the friend of the other, unless both love each other?

M: The latter certainly seems to be the case, Socrates.

S: If so, I continued, we think differently now from what we did before. Then it appeared that if one loved, both were friends, but now, that unless both love, neither are friends.

M: Yes. I'm afraid we have contradicted ourselves.

S: This being the case, then, the lover is not a friend to anything that does not love him in return.

M: Apparently not.[1]

One feels a bit sorry for poor Menexenus, whose head must certainly have been swimming, but Socrates' basic point is clear: friendship is a reciprocal or mutual love. And indeed, we would think it strange to speak of me as your friend simply on the grounds that I was deeply attached to you if that affection were in no way returned. To realize how peculiar this would be we need only call to mind the all-too-common picture of the outsider who attaches himself to "our group," indeed clings to us though we care not a whit for him and regularly refuse to incorporate him into our circle. It would be puzzling to call him our friend, however devoted his attachment to us may be.

It seems a simple matter of common sense to describe friendship as a reciprocal love. And any love so described may need to be questioned when our self-understanding is shaped by words such as these: "Love your enemies and pray for those who persecute you. . . . For if you love those who love you, what reward have you? . . . And if you salute only your brethren, what more are you doing than others?" (Matthew 5:44-47). If Christian love is directed always and only to the "neighbor," how can it discern and distinguish friends and enemies? In approaching friendship as a reciprocal love, therefore, we turn to another issue—like preference —in which philia and agape may seem to stand in stark contrast.[2]

I

The longer we probe this contrast, however, the more qualifications may seem necessary. The suggestion that a love which is purely self-giving must be higher than a love which, like friendship, requires reciprocity, though not entirely mistaken, warrants our examination. We can begin to see what is suspect about such a view if we examine it in a relatively strong and undiluted form. A good case study is Epistle IX of Seneca, the great Stoic philosopher and political advisor to Nero.[3]

Central to Seneca's discussion is the question of *need.* Is there something deficient about a human being who would admit that he needs friendship, needs to have his love returned? Seneca begins his letter by making that the issue:

> You desire to know whether Epicurus is right when, in one of his letters, he rebukes those who hold that the wise man is self-sufficient and for that reason does not stand in need of friendship.

In reply Seneca is willing to grant that the sage, though self-sufficient, may desire friends. To be sure, he can do without them, but he need not want to do without them. Of course, we may rightly be puzzled at how it should be that one who is self-sufficient nevertheless desires friends. Such desire seems to suggest a lack which would be out of place in a truly self-sufficient person. Sensing this, Seneca offers an explanation. The wise man desires friends, he writes, "if only for the purpose of practising friendship, in order that his noble qualities may not lie dormant." Whether anyone ever wished to be loved in friendship for that reason we may well wonder! Indeed, reading these words it is hard to be certain that Seneca is discussing anything we would be willing to call friendship.

Seneca proceeds to contrast his view with that of Epicurus, that ancient philosopher who was considered to have grounded all our actions (and, hence, also our friendships) in self-regarding motives. Epicurus, in one of his letters, suggests that even the wise man will need friends "that there may be someone to sit by him when he is ill, to help him when he is in prison or in want." Seneca cites this only to reverse it. Instead, he suggests, the wise man will desire friends "that he may have someone by whose sick-bed he himself may sit, someone a prisoner in hostile hands whom he himself may set free." To those of us who have heard countless times—and who believe—that "love seeks not its own," Seneca's view may seem more praiseworthy than Epicurus's. And surely Seneca is not wrong to point out that a friendship begun purely for the sake of advantage is not likely to be lasting. "The beginning and the end cannot but harmonize. He who begins to be your friend because it pays will also cease because it pays."

It may be, however, that the longer we place side by side the beliefs of Seneca and Epicurus the more convinced we may become that there is something inhumane about the Stoic view when compared with the Epicurean. To desire a friend in order that we may practice our virtue upon him is not really to love a friend. To desire a friend even in order that we may have someone to care for in time of need or danger is not yet to love a friend; it is to place one's self in the center of one's concern. Seneca's wise man "is in want of nothing, and yet needs many things." What this means, in fact, is that "he will live happily even without friends." The inhumanity of this becomes clear when Seneca considers a possible response to his view of the self-sufficiency of the sage.

People may say: "But what sort of existence will the wise man have, if he be left friendless when thrown into prison, or when stranded in some foreign nation, or when delayed on a long voyage, or when cast upon a lonely shore?" His life will be like that of Jupiter, who, amid the dissolution of the world, when the gods are confounded together and Nature rests for a space from her work, can retire into himself and give himself over to his own thoughts. In some such way as this the sage will act; he will retreat into himself, and live with himself.

Were they our only alternatives, it would be far more humane—because far more in keeping with our nature—simply to affirm with Epicurus that "the first cause of friendship was a man's needs."[4]

Love does not seek its own—but, at the very least, it cannot be indifferent to its own. We are, in the deepest recesses of our being, needy creatures, and to ask us to be indifferent to that need is to denigrate an essential element in our created nature. Seneca gives us a striking illustration of his ideal in the story of Stilbo, whose country was captured, whose children and wife were lost, and who

as he emerged from the general desolation alone and yet happy, spoke as follows to Demetrius, called Sacker of Cities because of the destruction he brought upon them, in answer to the question whether he had lost anything: "I have all my goods with me!"

That sacrifice in a good cause may be demanded of any of us we need not deny. That such sacrifice would involve no loss, that "alone and yet happy" we should respond, "I have all my goods with me!"—that we can and should deny. If, as Seneca reports in his letter, Epicurus was critical of Stilbo, then we must say that it was the Epicurean, not the Stoic, who had a firmer grasp on what it means to be a human being. For part of being human is being needy—in want of union with others and, ultimately, with God.

Friendship, a reciprocal and mutual love, recognizes this truth about our nature: that we need not only to give ourselves in love but also to receive love in return; that human beings are not meant, like Jupiter, to retreat into themselves and live with themselves alone. In failing to recognize this, the Stoic view cuts short the dynamic power which, as we noted in the previous chapter, is integral to the Augustinian understanding of love. If the friend fails to satisfy fully the longing of our hearts, the Stoic will view this as evidence that we were fundamentally mistaken to regard ourselves as needy. He will advise us to retreat into the self and become self-sufficient. And, of course, that is one possible response to a friendship which does not fully satisfy our longings. Its weakness, however, is that it hardens itself against that "shudder" before beauty which Plato had discerned and, in so doing, calls a premature halt to the quest of the restless heart. Premature and, still more, destructive of our humanity; for it is true, as C. S. Lewis wrote, that "the only place outside Heaven where you can be perfectly safe from all the dangers and perturbations of love is Hell."[5] Admitting our desire for *mutual* love which fulfills and satisfies our needy nature is a step toward admitting our need for God. This insight the Stoic declines—and is the poorer for it.

II

We began with the suggestion that a stark contrast between agape and a reciprocal love like friendship was perhaps overdone. Now, however, we may be in danger of making too little of the contrast, forgetting that there are good reasons why Christian thought has continually struggled with the problem of reciprocity in love. It is not accidental that such mutuality has often been regarded as suspect. "Love seeks not its own," the apostle wrote, and Christian conscience, instructed by those words, has sometimes wanted to say with Kierkegaard that "the true lover regards the very requirement of reciprocity to be a contamination, a devaluation, and loving without the reward of reciprocated love to be the highest blessedness."[6]

Kierkegaard contends that the "royal law," in making love a duty ("You *shall* love") has protected love against this contamination of reciprocity. Love which has "undergone the transformation of the eternal by becoming duty" continues to love regardless of any return or lack of return (p. 49). It remains unshakeable and unchangeable in every circumstance. It loves even the enemy, from whom of course no loving return is to be expected.

That this position is not without its own dangers we can see in those moments when Kierkegaard can sound a great deal like Seneca. He asks, for example,

who is stronger, he who says, "If you do not love me, I will hate you," or he who says, "If you hate me, I will still continue to love you?" (P. 49)

And we notice how, in such a passage, his central focus has subtly shifted. Here is Seneca's sage looking for opportunity to practice his virtue. The focus here is not upon how a love which has undergone the transformation of the eternal by becoming duty can better love and serve the neighbor. No, the focus is upon how such a love protects the lover, secures the lover in an independence which absolutely nothing can shake. The lover is stronger, says Kierkegaard. Like Jupiter, Seneca might add.

In other moments, however, Kierkegaard expresses his point differently and in a way which avoids these dangers. If the lover receives no return from the beloved, if the beloved is lost, shall the lover despair? The lover ought to *sorrow*, Kierkegaard replies, but not *despair*. He sorrows, because he is dependent on the beloved and (though Kierkegaard is always hesitant to put it this way) desires that his love be returned. He does not despair, because his love has been transformed by the eternal.

> I do not have the right to harden myself against the pains of life, for I *ought* to sorrow; but neither have I the right to despair, for I *ought* to sorrow; . . . So it is also with love. You have no right to harden yourself against this emotion, for you *ought* to love; but neither do you have the right to love despairingly, for you *ought* to love. . . . (P. 57)

What Augustine had achieved by conceiving of love as a power whose inherent dynamism draws the lover on toward God, Kierkegaard here achieves by understanding love as a duty. Disappointment in love, a lack of reciprocity, are to be taken not as an invitation to retreat like Jupiter into the self but to remain faithful in love. For it is a duty to do so. Though Augustine's and Kierkegaard's ways of achieving this end are quite different, and though we might disagree at length about which is the better or more successful, each demonstrates that Christian thought cannot make reciprocity a required feature of all love. A mutual love like friendship, however important for human life and well-being, cannot stand alone. Christian thought knows also a love which does not seek its own. The trick is to learn how to relate these two seemingly different loves. Augustine did it, we have seen, by viewing a love like friendship as preparation for and intimation of the greater love of charity, and then in turn viewing a transformed friendship as the internal fruition of charity. How Kierkegaard relates these loves, and whether he does so persuasively, is harder to say.

"Love believes all things," the apostle writes, and Kierkegaard suggests that, taking this seriously, we will be helped to see why a requirement of reciprocity in love is questionable. Suppose we offer love to someone, expecting to be loved in return. And suppose that expectation *seems* to be fulfilled. Still, we may be mistaken. The supposed friend may deliberately deceive us. But once think of that—we may be deceived—and the thought is a paralyzing one for the would-be lover. What if I give myself and receive in return only the appearance but not the reality of love? Perhaps I should not give myself. Perhaps a kind of mistrust of the other, an attitude incompatible with love, is really the wisest course to follow lest I be deceived in love.

Reflecting in this way Kierkegaard is led once again to question the place of reciprocity in love. By loving in this way, he suggests, "one makes a transaction of love" (p. 223). By contrast, the "true lover," as Kierkegaard likes to call him, can never be deceived. For, expecting and requiring nothing in return, how can he ever be deceived? How can he ever be led to wonder whether his love has been returned in reality or only in appearance? The true lover simply abides in love, believing all things. Speaking in our ordinary sense, this lover may of course suspect that he is being deceived. "But he knows that deception and truth stretch equally far and that consequently it still is possible that the deceiver is not a deceiver, and therefore he believes all things" (p. 229). Kierkegaard's insight here is sure: Begin to concern oneself with the possibility of deception, begin with mistrust rather than acceptance in love, and there is no way to break free of such mistrust. After all, what appears to be deception may not be, and what appears to be truth may be only sophisticated deception. Begin by taking reciprocity as our central concern and we will be ineluctably forced by the truth of this insight to retreat into the self, trusting no one and giving ourselves to no one.

Here again Kierkegaard sometimes presses his point too far—or gives it a sudden twist—and sounds disconcertingly like Seneca. There is a large difference between saying that love believes all things in its wholehearted devotion to the neighbor and saying that since love is never deceived the true lover is secure against being mistaken. At times Kierkegaard's concern seems to be the latter rather than the former. In such moments we get the unpleasant feeling that love is being turned into a weapon with which to protect the self against the possibility of rejection—a tactic all of us are familiar with from our own experience. Kierkegaard can, for example, write that

> one who believes all things can very easily give the appearance of a poor abandoned wretch whom every one can deceive, and yet he is the only one who is eternally and infinitely secured against being deceived. (P. 229)

Or again, he can suggest that, precisely by refusing to ask the slightest reciprocity, "the true lover has assumed an unassailable position" (p. 228).

But the point, I had thought, was not for the lover to secure himself or acquire a position which could not be assailed. The point had been simply to love neighbors without demanding anything in return, with a love that seeks not its own and believes all things. The suddenness and ease with which Kierkegaard can shift from a focus on the neighbor to a focus on protecting the self serves as a reminder that it will never be satisfactory to remove from our concept of love those elements which express our neediness—elements like friendship's reciprocity. Remove them and that neediness will only reassert itself in new, less desirable ways—most often in the Stoic attempt to find some path to self-sufficiency. To deny our neediness is to try to live a lie, and it must inevitably deny important features of our common nature.

Perhaps one of Kierkegaard's finest attempts to give expression to his viewpoint—and to suggest how loves like philia and agape may interpenetrate—comes in his example of how one might "pack his whole life together in a dash" (p. 259). In this context he is speaking not merely of friendship but of many different human loves, among which friendship may well claim an important place. The very best thing one person can do for another, he suggests, is to care for the other in such a way that it would be true to say, "he stands alone—by my help" (p. 256).

> There are many writers who employ dashes on every occasion of thought-failure, and there are also those who use dashes with sensitivity and taste. But a dash has truly never been used more significantly than in the little sentence above. . . . For in this little sentence the infinity of thought is contained in the most profound way, the greatest contradiction overcome. He stands alone—this is the highest; he stands alone—nothing else do you see. You see no aid or assistance, no awkward bungler's hand holding on to him any more than it occurs to the person himself that someone has helped him. No, he stands alone—by another's help. But this help is hidden, . . . it is hidden behind a dash. (Pp. 256f.)

We can make the point, less poetically to be sure, in this way: To say that we cannot be happy or fulfilled unless our love is reciprocated may well be true. Indeed, it is important to say this if only to be clear that we really are needy creatures, not self-sufficient gods. But what we need and desire in friendship is not merely the return of our love. We need a relation of both giving and receiving between free and equal participants. To give only for the sake of getting a return must poison the relationship from the outset. And the same is true of giving in such a way that the other is not left free to reject our offer of friendship. To give without such conditions will, no doubt, entail the risk that our love may not come to its fruition in friendship, but that is a risk which any genuine friendship must, by its very nature, be willing to run. Hence, admitting our need for mutual love, we must nevertheless love in a way which is not dependent on any return. Our neediness, though not denied, must be hidden behind a dash. To seek one's own is the surest way to miss it. And a love that seeks not its own is a prerequisite to mutuality. It is an old but true paradox that only the one who loses his life finds it. Josef Pieper summarizes the matter nicely. ⌐/

> That love, insofar as it is real love, does not seek its own remains an inviolable truth. But the lover, assuming that he is disinterested and not calculating, does after all attain his own, the reward of love. And this reward, in its turn, and in view of human nature cannot be a matter of indifference to him.[7]

What Kierkegaard has given us is a new insight into the complex relationship between philia and agape. In the previous chapter, discussing preference in love, I suggested that the standpoint of Augustine—seeing preferential love as intimation of and preparation for love of God and the neighbor-in-God—is more persuasive than Kierkegaard's attempt to ground all preferential loves in agapeic neighbor-love. But now, when considering the reciprocal character of love, there is a good bit to be said for what Kierkegaard implies: that rather than thinking simply of a gradual progression from one form of love to another, we must also try to see these loves as necessarily intermingled from the outset. Without the self-giving spirit of Kierkegaard's "true lover," genuine friendship can be neither created nor sustained. The lover must hide behind the dash, demanding nothing in return. And at the same time, without a willingness to admit our neediness and to *sorrow* when mutual love is not sustained, the glad receptivity of friendship must be lacking. The reciprocal love of friendship, though of enormous significance for human life, is not able to support itself. Underlying it must be the selflessness which is not ashamed to receive and which, while giving, is glad to hide behind the dash.

III

Most of the problems we experience in discussing the place of reciprocity in love arise from the tension between two elements, neither of which can be eliminated from our concept of love. Love includes both wishing the other well for the other's sake and desiring union with the other. And that rather abstract language can cloak the difficulties of holding these together coherently. If we demand the return of fellowship from the one we love, we no longer affirm that loved one for his or her sake alone. And yet, a mere affirmation of the other person without any desire for enjoyment of the presence of that person seems too impersonal to do justice to our concept of love.

This desire to enjoy the friend ought not be identified with ordinary self-interested behavior. We desire to enjoy the *friend*, not the pleasure which accompanies the presence of the friend. St. Thomas Aquinas distinguishes between love of desire (*amor concupiscentiae*) and what he calls the love of friendship (*amor amicitiae*).[8] By the latter he means essentially a disinterested love which simply wills what is good for another person. Contrasted with this is the love of desire, his example being when we love a wine. Hence, what Thomas calls *amor amicitiae* is simply *amor benevolentiae*, a benevolent love. But this means that—in order to make clear that friendship is not self-interested— Thomas has come close to suggesting that the love of friendship regards reciprocity as unnecessary. He seeks to avoid this by suggesting later that good will (*benevolentia*) alone is not sufficient for friendship, which requires mutual loving or reciprocal good will. And, in accordance with his stated belief that charity is a kind of friendship, Thomas can then say that "love, as an act of charity, includes good will but adds to it a union of the affections."[9]

Good will *and* a union of the affections. Neither can be eliminated from love if our concept and experience of love are not to suffer impoverishment. If we eliminate good will, we are hard pressed to suggest how the enemy should be loved. If we eliminate union of the affections, we have little reason to desire that the enemy become a friend. Indeed, we cannot, I think, even make either of these predominant without skewing what we say about love. St. Thomas himself falls prey to this danger. Attempting to explain charity as a kind of friendship, he must necessarily give greater place in his explanation to the union of affections, since friendship is so clearly a reciprocal love. But how then, he asks, can charity extend even to our enemies, who obviously make no return? Thomas's reply is that friendship may be said to be extended in one of two ways: (1) when the friend is loved in himself, or (2) when he is loved for the sake of some other person (e.g., as when we love the children of a friend).[10] Therefore, he suggests, the friendship of charity extends to the enemy when we love him for the sake of God. True enough, one is inclined to say, but not quite friendship in any ordinary sense of the term. This is more like Aristotle's "inactive friendship," simple good will.

We have, then, two elements in love: benevolence and the desire to enjoy the other person in a reciprocal union of the affections. Neither can be eliminated. Neither can be given pride of place over the other. The relationships between these elements are as complex as human interactions. Friendship with some people may begin to fashion us into the sort of persons who will feel and exercise benevolence toward many others. Friendship may also be the internal fruition—long awaited perhaps—of a love which began purely as benevolence. And there may be benevolent love which is never reciprocated, which never comes to such fruition, since the enemy may never become a friend. Both elements in love are integral to our humanity. We ought not give up the desire for mutual love and try to be Stoics. Neither ought we permit our love to be limited to the small circle of those who return it. And, while avoiding any premature reconciliation of these two loves within the brokenness of human history, we may rightfully hope that "the divine power which bears history can complete what even the highest human striving must leave incomplete."[11] We may, that is, hope for a day and a community in which good will is regularly crowned in mutual love, its internal fruition.

If we seek to press beyond this, theological ethics can do no more than suggest what we learned from Kierkegaard above: that a spirit of self-giving must underlie both genuine good will for another person and the desire that one's love be returned. If Christian thought correctly discerns in our prideful desire to be independent the fundamental sin of our nature, neither of these will come naturally for us. To affirm and commit ourselves to the well-being of another person, even when there is little hope of return on that commitment, goes beyond what we can manage much of the time. Nor is a glad receptivity, free of any desire to receive solely on our own terms, something of which we are often capable. Neither element can be fully what it is meant to be, neither can be whole, unless it is transformed by that self-giving spirit which is, I think, the fundamental meaning of Christian agape.

The love commandment given Christians reaches its zenith in the fifteenth chapter of John's Gospel, where Jesus instructs his disciples in a love which goes considerably beyond any Golden Rule. "This is my commandment, that you love one another as I have loved you. Greater love has no man than this, that a man lay down his life for his friends" (John 15:12f.). Love, as Jesus advocates and lives it, means in Arthur McGill's words, *self-expenditure* for another's need."[12] That such self-giving leads to life and self-fulfillment is God's own secret, hidden in the mystery of his being and announced in the vindication of Jesus in the resurrection. Thus, even if we cannot fully reconcile the claims of benevolence and reciprocity, we can say that each requires for its completion the self-giving spirit which comes from being taken up into Christ—and thereby into the life of God which is love. If we really want a simple religion of love, G. K. Chesterton once wrote, we will have to look for it in the Athanasian Creed.[13] And while it may seem strange, it is true that we cannot discuss friendship adequately without driving our discussion back to the trinitarian life of God. In that divine life the Father eternally begets the Son—that is to say, eternally affirms the being of the Son. The Son, eternally receptive, receives that begotten life and offers it back, returns it to the Father. And the Spirit is the bond of their love, the Spirit of their self-giving. For it is self-giving that makes possible the Father's affirmation of the Son, and it is likewise self-giving which makes possible the Son's glad receptivity. Even here love seeks not its own.

To say that God is love is to say that such a Spirit of self-giving makes possible the fellowship that God is— makes possible both benevolence and a union of the affections. We can understand why St. Thomas wanted to call charity a form of friendship; for even if that is not exactly the case, it is true that mutual love is the internal fruition of charity in the Godhead. In order to be God, the Father's good will, eternally expressed in the begetting of the Son, needs to be crowned in the return of that love by the Son—and it is the Spirit of self-giving which unites Father and Son and makes this possible.

The golden apple of selfhood, thrown among the false gods, became an apple of discord because they scrambled for it. They did not know the first rule of the holy game, which is that every player must by all means touch the ball and then immediately pass it on. To be found with it in your hands is a fault: to cling to it, death. But when it

flies to and fro among the players too swift for eye to
follow, and the great master Himself leads the revelry,
giving Himself eternally to His creatures in the genera-
tion, and back to Himself in the sacrifice, of the Word,
then indeed the eternal dance "makes heaven drowsy with
the harmony."[14]

Friendship as a reciprocal affection cannot be the whole
truth about love. Underlying and sustaining it must be
a self-giving spirit. But only an impoverished theological vision—and an impoverished understanding of
human nature—could deny mutual love an important
place as the hoped-for internal fruition of all love.

3. Friendship and Fidelity

Does the dance cease because one dancer has gone away? In a certain sense. But if the other still remains standing in the posture which expresses a turning towards the one who is not seen, and if you know nothing about the past, then you will say, "Now the dance will begin just as soon as the other comes, the one who is expected."

Kierkegaard, *Works of Love*

We have explored in previous chapters two of the essential characteristics of the love of friendship. It is a preferential and a reciprocal love. Christian love, though not entirely incompatible with friendship, is in itself neither preferential nor reciprocal. Out of that fact grow the tensions we have discussed. We turn now to a third such tension, one which arises inevitably out of the previous two.

Friendship is not love in general; rather, it is a deep attachment to and preference for another person because of the sort of person he or she is. Yet, because this is the case, it seems necessary to say that if one of the persons changes, the relationship must change and friendship may die. If friendship is preferential love, it must cease when the characteristics which gave rise to such preference are no longer present. And if the affection of friendship fails and fades in either party, then one can only admit that the reciprocal and mutually

shared good will which friendship involves is gone.
Friendship, in order to be friendship—that is, in order
to be a preferential and reciprocal love—must be subject
to change.

Not so with Christian love. It is determined not by
the characteristics of the loved one nor by any antici-
pated return but solely by its own self-giving character.
"How can I give you up, O Ephraim!" Yahweh cries out
through his prophet (Hosea 11:9). And the Evangelist
depicts the standard for agape when he writes of Jesus
that "having loved his own who were in the world, he
loved them to the end" (John 13:1). The God who in
nature has faithfully made his sun to rise on evil and
good and sent his rain on just and unjust (Matthew
5:45) is thereby claimed to have proven himself just as
faithful within history. It is not surprising that such
love should make neither preference nor reciprocity
central. Agape, in order to be agape—that is, in order
to be a faithful love—must, it seems, be nonpreferential
and unconcerned with reciprocity.

Perhaps, therefore, we ought simply to face the harsh
truth to which this brief analysis gives rise: friendship
and fidelity are incompatible. We can purchase permanence in love only by sacrificing the delights of
preference and reciprocity, and we can enjoy friendship
only by sacrificing the assurance of permanence. And
yet, it is not clear that either of these is precisely what
we desire. "A friend loves at all times" (Proverbs 17:17).
That is what we want: faithful friendship. The hard
question is whether we can have it.

I

It should be no surprise that certain friendships cease.
Those ties, for example, which were based solely on the
usefulness of the friends to each other are not likely to
survive a change in circumstances which makes obso-

lete the mutually advantageous relationship which existed. Plutarch put the point well.

> In the house of rich men and rulers, the people see a noisy throng of visitors offering their greetings and shaking hands and playing the part of armed retainers, and they think that those who have so many friends must be happy. Yet they can see a far greater number of flies in those persons' kitchens. But the flies do not stay on after the good food is gone, nor the retainers after their patron's usefulness is gone.[1]

And even in the case of character-friendships, if these are formed before young people reach some degree of maturity, we are neither surprised nor even particularly dismayed to discover that those who were once close friends have grown apart and fallen out of touch. Where character is not yet relatively formed, character-friendship must necessarily be unstable.

Far more tragic, yet also understandable, are friendships which falter when the friends find themselves in unalterable disagreement on some good greater even than friendship itself. If, as I argued when discussing the preferential character of friendship, the exclusiveness of friendship is meant to lead on to a more all-embracing form of community, we have to reckon with the possibility that a more universal good may, at any time, demand our loyalty in an overriding way. Thus Aristotle, referring to his friendship for the author of the Theory of Ideas, which he is criticizing, says that truth must be valued more highly even than friendship —a sentiment which would surely have been understood by the author of that theory who himself had written that "we must not honor a man above truth."[2]

Indeed, in Christian terms one must always presume at least one such qualification to be written into friendship: namely, that loyalty to the friend could not override faithfulness to God, if these should seem to conflict. Thus, Aelred of Rievaulx, in perhaps the most important treatise on friendship to emerge from medieval monastic life, could write:

> It is clear, then, . . . what the fixed and true limit of
> spiritual friendship is: namely, that nothing ought to be
> denied to a friend, nothing ought to be refused for a friend,
> which is less than the very precious life of the body, which
> divine authority has taught should be laid down for a
> friend. Hence, since the life of the soul is of far greater
> excellence than that of the body, any action, we believe,
> should be altogether denied a friend which brings about
> the death of the soul, that is, sin, which separated God
> from the soul and the soul from life.[3]

In a rather different literary vein, Dorothy Sayers explores such a conflict in *Unnatural Death*, one of her Lord Peter Wimsey stories. Mary Whittaker, a murderess, is using Vera Findlater to provide her with an alibi. Vera is an extremely devoted and loyal friend (who mistakenly believes that the same is true of Mary) and has permitted ties of personal loyalty to lead her to lie on Mary's behalf. In a conversation with Miss Climpson, who seems an innocuous spinster but is really investigating for Lord Peter, the theological issue is raised.

> "But a great friendship does make demands," cried Miss
> Findlater eagerly. "It's got to be just everything to one.
> It's wonderful the way it seems to colour all one's thoughts.
> Instead of being centred in oneself, one's centred in the
> other person. That's what Christian love means—one's
> ready to die for the other person."
> "Well, I don't know," said Miss Climpson. "I once heard
> a sermon about that from a most *splendid* priest—and he
> said that that kind of love might become *idolatry* if one
> wasn't very careful. He said that Milton's remark about
> Eve—you know, 'he for God only, she for God in him'—
> was not congruous with Catholic doctrine. One must get
> the *proportions* right, and it was *out of proportion* to see
> everything through the eyes of another fellow-creature."[4]

To prefer the friend above God, who gives the friend, would be an inordinate love—one in which, as Miss

Climpson's splendid priest put it, the proportions were not right. And, however tragic the choice might be on certain occasions, one must be willing to say to the friend what the Cavalier poet said to a different kind of beloved in conflict with a lesser god "I could not love thee dear, loved I not honor more."

Conflicts such as these are not the chief obstacle to faithful friendship. That barrier is something far less heroic-sounding, far more mundane. "The most fatal disease of friendship," Dr. Johnson wrote, "is gradual decay."[5] Perhaps time heals all wounds, but only by teaching forgetfulness of the wounds which time itself inflicts. We are temporal beings, constantly changing. And a love like friendship, which depends so greatly on shared interests and enjoyments, is easily weakened or destroyed by altered circumstances. Any change in our circumstances, our vocation, our education, our wealth will slowly have its effect on our friendships. New enjoyments and interests crowd out old ones—crowding out also thereby the friendships built on those old enjoyments and interests. The measured sentences of Dr. Johnson come to terms with the humble realities of finite existence.

> Many have talked, in very exalted language, of the perpetuity of friendship, of invincible constancy, and unalienable kindness; and some examples have been seen of men who have continued faithful to their earliest choice; and whose affection has predominated over changes of fortune, and contrariety of opinion.
>
> But these instances are memorable, because they are rare. The friendship which is to be practised or expected by common mortals, must take its rise from mutual pleasure, and must end when the power ceases of delighting each other.

Hence, Dr. Johnson suggests, "there is no human possession of which the duration is less certain." Insofar as our experience suggests this to be accurate, it merely confirms what sober analysis of the requirements of friendship and the requirements of fidelity suggests: that faithful friendship is likely to be very rare in human experience. Friendship involves the delights and enjoyments which preference and reciprocity make possible. Fidelity requires a steadfastness of purpose which perseveres even when none of those enjoyments is present.

It remains open to us to respond to this pessimistic forecast in different ways. Aristotle, for example, accepts with sober realism the fact that friendships may be dissolved. He discusses the possibility that the character of one friend may change for the worse or that one person may remain what he was while the other becomes better and a far superior person.[6] If the character of a friend becomes evil, he suggests, the friendship should not be broken off at once, but if the change seems unlikely to be reversed, "no one would regard a person who breaks off such a friendship as acting strangely. . . . His friend has changed, and since he is unable to save him, he severs his connections with him." Likewise, if one simply becomes far superior to the other and "the distance between them becomes great," it is impossible that friendship should be sustained. Aristotle does not regard this as likely to happen in friendships among mature adults, since he regards character as habitual and unlikely to change, but he recognizes the possibility in quite matter-of-fact fashion. Even such a realistic view cannot deny, however, that the commitments which friendship involves continue to have claims on us.

> Should, then, a former friend be treated just as if he had never been a friend at all? No; we should remember our past familiarity with him, and just as we feel more obliged to do favors for friends than for strangers, we must show some consideration to him for old friendship's sake, provided that it was not excessive wickedness on his part that broke the friendship.

Cicero, in his equally famous treatise on friendship, agrees that if friendships end they should "appear to have burned out rather than to have been stamped out." [7] Yet, even while recognizing that friendships may fade and that new friends may be preferred to old, Cicero is less willing than Aristotle to acquiesce in this fact of life. "There should be no surfeit of friendships as there is of other things; and, as in the case of wines that improve with age, the oldest friendships ought to be the most delightful . . ." (XIX, 67). There we hear the desire for faithful friendship again given voice. Friendship should not die; for it involves more than common interests, enjoyments, and purposes. It is also a relation of deep intimacy and loyalty, involving such deep commitment and sharing that it calls for permanence.

II

If friendship's duration is so uncertain, one may well ask whether there is any way to protect friendship against dissolution. And there is one answer, often given by those who have written on friendship, which deserves to be taken seriously if only because it has been given so frequently: test the prospective friend in advance of proffering friendship. Emerson—whose essay on friendship is considerably overrated and whose "the only way to have a friend is to be one" sounds quite different when read in context—states the typical view concisely and eloquently: "Let us buy our entrance to this guild by a long probation." [8]

Cicero, living in an age when friendships were of political and not merely private importance, develops the theme of testing at great length. It is wise, he suggests, to "exercise such care in forming friendships that we should never begin to love anyone whom we might sometime hate" (XVI, 60). A qualification, one is constrained to reply, which may severely limit the circle of one's potential friends! The more detail Cicero gives us about what he has in mind, the more uncomfortable, we may become.

It is the part of wisdom to check the headlong rush of goodwill as we would that of a chariot, and thereby so manage friendship that we may in some degree put the dispositions of friends, as we do those of horses, to a preliminary test. Some men often give proof in a petty money transaction how unstable they are; while others, who could not have been influenced by a trivial sum, are discovered in one that is large. (XVII, 63)

One feels instinctively that there is something unsatisfactory—perhaps even repugnant—about such a notion; yet most of us do so test those with whom we are in danger of becoming "too close."[9]

We can, however, move beyond an initial, undeveloped reaction to Cicero's view of the necessity of testing; for there is a fundamental flaw in his suggestion, a flaw to which his own discussion points. He suggests a problem but does not pursue it.

We ought, therefore, to choose men who are firm, steadfast and constant, a class of which there is a great dearth; and at the same time it is very hard to come to a decision without a trial, while such trial can only be made in actual friendship: thus friendship outruns the judgment and takes away the opportunity of a trial. (XVII, 62)

Friendships, if there are to be any at all, must be formed before we can have any certain knowledge that the other person is truly lovable, one suited for our friendship. This means that we may commit ourselves to persons for whom our regard may fade. Yet, in thus committing ourselves to another person, we create in that friend a set of expectations, needs, and loyalties which cannot simply be set aside without pain and grief. Again we see that the bond of friendship seems to call for a permanence which it cannot itself provide. Try to avoid making mistakes in friendship and we will have no friends at all. Acquire the necessary experience which only friendship and some "mistaken judgments" can provide and in so doing we make commitments and establish expectations which call for fidelity. Can the tension between friendship and fidelity be overcome? When discussing reciprocity in friendship I suggested that the self-giving of agape may be a necessary component of friendship from the very outset, that without such self-giving no mutual love could spring up or be sustained. That provided a convenient way to suggest that agape and philia do not only stand in tension; rather, it is equally true to suggest that the natural love of friendship stands in need of agape, that it is supported and sustained by a love which is not natural to the creature. It would be nice if in discussing the tension between friendship and fidelity we could do the same, but we cannot.

Aelred of Rievaulx, for example, wants to hold that true friendship can never cease. He has as authorities, after all, the scriptural passage that "a friend loves at all times" as well as a statement of Jerome's which he cites: "friendship which can end, was never true friendship." But in attempting to explain how this can be possible, Aelred is driven to a viewpoint which seems implausible. He distinguishes four elements in a bond of friendship—love (by which he means benevolence and good will), affection, security (i.e., trust), and happiness. He grants that a friendship burdened with various difficulties may come to lose affection, security, and happiness. Hence, he concludes, "that familiarity, in which such things find their place, must be denied to a former friend, but love should not be withdrawn. . . ."[10] What we have left, of course, is a bond that is neither preferential nor reciprocal—mere good will. That can last, to be sure, but it is hard to see why we should call it friendship.

We can probe the tension between friendship and fidelity more deeply if we consider what may be the most striking passage in a very striking book—Kierkegaard's *Works of Love*. St. Paul writes that "love abides," and in the light of that Kierkegaard considers the possibility of a rupture in love.

And so the breaking-point between the two is reached. It was a misunderstanding; yet one of them broke the relationship. But the lover says, "I abide"—therefore there still is no break. Imagine a compound word which lacks the last word; there is only the first word and the hyphen (for the one who breaks the relationship still cannot take the hyphen with him; the lover naturally keeps the hyphen on his side); imagine, then, the first word and the hyphen of a compound word, and now imagine that you know absolutely nothing more about how it hangs together—what will you say? You will say that the word is not complete, that it lacks something. It is the same with the lover. That the relationship has reached the breaking-point cannot be seen directly; it can be known only from the angle of the past. But the lover wills not to know the past, for he abides; and to abide is in the direction of the future. Consequently the lover expresses that the relationship which another considers broken is a relationship which has not yet been completed. . . . What a difference there is between a fragment and an unfinished sentence! In order to call something a fragment, one must know that nothing more is to come. If one does not know this, he says that the sentence is not yet completed. . . . But suppose now that it is three years since that they last spoke together. See, here it comes again. That it was three years ago one can know only in the sense of the past; but the lover, who daily renews himself by the eternal and abides, over him the past has no power at all. If you saw two persons sitting silent together and you knew nothing more, would you thereby conclude that it was three years since they spoke together? Can any one determine how long a silence must have been in order to say now, there is no more conversation; and if one can determine this, in a particular instance one can nevertheless know only from the angle of the past whether this is so, for the time must indeed be past. But the lover, who abides, continually emancipates himself from his knowledge of the past; he knows no past; he waits only for the future.[11]

The lover keeps the hyphen. Perhaps no one has ever pictured so magnificently the meaning of steadfastness in love. But clearly, it must be agape, not philia, which Kierkegaard here describes. Imagine a friendship in which neither friend has spoken for three years. To call such a bond a friendship would be contrary to what almost everyone who has written on friendship has thought it necessary to say: that friends long to spend time together; that friends want to share their interests and enjoyments with one another.

There may be deep commitment to the well-being of the neighbor in the love Kierkegaard describes, but we should not call it friendship. And, of course, Kierkegaard himself understands this quite well. He contrasts what it means to love "the neighbor" with what it means to love a friend or a beloved.

> The beloved can treat you in such a way that he is lost to you, and you can lose a friend, but whatever a neighbour does to you, you can never lose him. To be sure, you can also continue to love your beloved and your friend no matter how they treat you, but you cannot truthfully continue to call them beloved and friend when they, sorry to say, have really changed. No change, however, can take your neighbour from you, for it is not your neighbour who holds you fast—it is your love which holds your neighbour fast. (P. 76)

Here, as is very often the case with Kierkegaard, the very strength of his insight is also its greatest danger. It becomes too easy to suggest, as Kierkegaard himself does, that if the lover holds on to love even when the beloved ruptures their relationship, then "the break has no power over him" (p. 283). And that is quite different from saying that the lover keeps the hyphen. To say that the break has no power over the lover can too easily come to mean that the relationship was of little consequence, as if only the relation with the Eternal and not our fragile, earthly bonds were important. To say that the lover keeps the hyphen on his side, that he wills not to be determined by the past but, instead, to live for the future, is to admit the relationship is of enormous significance—for what love believes when it abides is that the relationship "has not yet been completed."

We have reached a point at which the difference between agape and philia must be plain. If friendship ceases, the steadfastness of love may still be directed toward that neighbor who once was friend, but agape cannot simply be substituted for friendship without loss. To say, "though I can no longer love him as a friend, I can continue in a self-giving spirit to be devoted to his good," may be very important indeed. But such a simple substitution of agape for philia must be understood to be just that—a substitution of one love for another, and a substitution in which something of great importance is lost.

We achieve permanence in love by ceasing to let our love be concerned with or determined by the particular character of the loved one. Friendship never loves that way. Friendship loves and prefers a particular person because of what that person is. That is why, when the person changes, friendship changes or fades. And though it may be good to know that we are loved with a love which never fades, it is doubtful whether anyone wishes to be loved in only that way—in spite of what we are, rather than because of what we are. No doubt that is better than not to be loved at all. But being loved in that way does not offer all that we need or want. To be loved with agape alone is, however important, not sufficient; for it is too impersonal. It is not surprising that the words "I love you despite your failings" should as often be a subtle weapon as a genuine affirmation of the other person.

The tension between philia and agape must be permitted to stand. Friendship, in order to be preferential and reciprocal, must be subject to change. Yet, a friendship which lacks permanence seems less than perfect. Agape, in order to be faithful, must be nonpreferential and unconcerned with reciprocity. Yet, a love which lacks these marks of philia—its deep intimacy, mutuality, and preference—seems too impersonal and cold to satisfy the needs of our nature.

III

Either our desire for faithful friendship is sheer self-delusion or else it is permissible to hope for a day and a community in which such friendship might become possible, to hope that temporality and change might lose their relentless power over our commitments. Agape, with its steadfastness, should enter into friendship to perfect it. Friendship, with its warmth and mutuality, should be the internal fruition of agape. It was sound theological instinct, not mere wish-fulfillment, which led medieval thinkers to conceive of heaven as a "vast friendship." Nothing less than this, a community in which friendship and charity are coextensive, will satisfy the needs of our nature. Nothing less than this will correspond to the mutuality of the triune life of God into which he wills to draw us.

Such a hope is expressed better by Augustine's vision of life as pilgrimage toward the enjoyment of God than Kierkegaard's sterner vision of love as duty brought about through transformation by the Eternal, a vision which tries too quickly to resolve the argument between philia and agape. To think of love solely as a duty does, to be sure, recognize that any love which is attached to the friend because of his character will be subject to change if that character changes. However, love as duty purchases permanence at the cost of mutuality. The eternal steadfastness of Christian love should not simply replace the mutuality of philia. If friendship ends, a willingness to serve and help must never be withdrawn, but one must also hope for something more. That something more is expressed in the vision of human life as pilgrimage toward the community God is fashioning. This more patient image permits us to take time and its terrors seriously without being overcome by them. It permits us to express better the complexities of relating philia and agape. Attachment to friends is a school in which we are trained for that greater community. Steadfast faithfulness in love is necessary even when friendship ceases. But faithful friendship is the goal—a goal which can be realized only when the friend is loved in God. To love the friend in God is not to love what is godlike in the friend—precisely at that point Christian thought parts company with the classical conception of friendship. Not the friend's goodness but the Goodness which possesses the friend and is refracted by the friend is what the eye is to discern. Only thus is the friend seen as God's creature and loved appropriately.

We cannot resolve the tension between friendship and fidelity; we can only state some of the truths to which reflection upon this tension gives rise. Life is a journey, a pilgrimage toward that community in which friends love one another in God and time no longer inflicts its wounds on friendship. Along the way, friendship is a school, training us in the meaning and enactment of love. Friendship is also a foretaste of the internal reciprocities of love which have yet to be fully realized. And, it is important to add, friendship is a good which may have to be sacrificed here and now in order to be fully realized in the sharing of the divine life.

But to speak of faithful friendship is to conjoin in hope what cannot be fully united within human history. Time is not that easily or quickly tamed by eternity, and one must learn to be patient. Such patience is possible, however, for those who believe that the changeable character of our friendships—the work of time—need not stand in irreconcilable tension with the steadfastness of love transformed by the Eternal. Cicero could do no more than point toward such a possibility.

How grievous and hard to most persons does association in another's misfortunes appear! Nor is it easy to find men who will go down to calamity's depths for a friend. . . .Whoever, therefore, in either of these contingencies, has shown himself staunch, immovable, and firm in friendship ought to be considered to belong to that class of men which is exceedingly rare—aye, almost divine. (XVII, 64)

Christian ethics affirms that such a love has entered history in Jesus of Nazareth and that this love is, to paraphrase Niebuhr, a tangent toward eternity in time.[12] The presence within history of such love justifies the Christian hope for faithful friendship. It is the reason for believing that, even if one partner in the dance turns away for a time, it is appropriate to remain standing in that posture which "expresses a turning towards the one who is not seen" and thereby says, "Now the dance will begin just as soon as the other comes, the one who is expected."

4. Politics and Ethics: Civic Friendship

> Politics is a second-rate form of activity . . . at once
> corrupting to the soul and fatiguing to the mind, the
> activity either of those who cannot live without the
> illusion of affairs or those so fearful of being ruled by
> others that they will pay away their lives to prevent it.
> Michael Oakeshott, *Rationalism in Politics*

In our society the private bond of friendship is usually regarded as far less important than the public bond of citizenship. And indeed, if the preferential character of friendship creates problems for Christian ethics, it is not difficult to see why the more universal bond of citizenship might have come to seem more deserving as a focus for our attention and activity.

In politics one often has not friends but comrades. Whereas friends need have no substantive purpose—they may simply share common interests and enjoy each other's company—comrades are joined in a relation less formal and more purposive. The lost comrade can be replaced; not so the lost friend. J. Glenn Gray has perceptively contrasted the two bonds in discussing the comradeship of men in battle. Indeed, he suggests that one of the "enduring appeals of battle" lies in the comradeship it creates, a comradeship in which we are liberated from our individual impotence and in which "individual fate loses its central importance."[1] Those who might never become friends may well become com-

68

rades if circumstances are right. But when these circumstances change and the battle ceases, the experience
of comradeship cannot be sustained. Friendship requires not the presence of danger nor, certainly,
organization for the achievement of a concrete goal. "Its
true domain is peace, only peace."[2] We are reminded of
a saying attributed to Epicurus, who exalted friendship
so highly: "Amid so many blessings, it has done us no
harm that our glorious Greece not only does not know
us, but has hardly heard of us."[3]

What disciplined Christian ethical reflection may
perhaps train us to see in this contrast is the *active*
quality of comradeship when contrasted with friendship. It would not do to say that the friendship bond is
self-regarding and comradeship other-regarding; to put
the matter that way would for Christian ethics determine their relative priority from the outset. On the
contrary, friendship is certainly an other-regarding
relationship even if, as Gray puts it, self-awareness is
heightened in friendship and suppressed in comradeship.[4] Even if both relationships are other-regarding,
however, it seems true to say that friendship—when
contrasted with comradeship—has about it something
of the character of a retreat. Genuine friendship will,
we noted in an earlier chapter, remain open to receiving
new friends, but when we contrast it with comradeship
we must probably grant that it is less active in seeking
out neighbors to serve, less universal in its focus of
concern. It may seem even frivolous, lacking the substantive purpose to which comrades are devoted. It is
possible, however, to blur the contrast between these
two bonds and speak of "civic friendship."

I

In his *Nicomachean Ethics* Aristotle writes that
friendship "seems to hold states together" (VIII, 1). He

expresses therein a feature of Greek thought far re-
moved from our own way of thinking. Since friendship
involves something held in common, Aristotle could
regard any bond which united people as an expression
of philia. He could, for example, discuss the family
relationship as a bond of friendship. Similarly, *homonoia*
(concord) within the political community is the social
expression of friendship, and citizens in a polis are
united by a bond of civic friendship. Aristotle writes, for
example, that "when people are friends, they have no
need of justice, but when they are just, they need friendship in addition" (VIII, 1). This view, which conceives
the civic bond primarily as one of philia, warrants our
consideration and investigation.

The history of the Greek city-state would suggest
that we ought not be too sanguine about the possibilities for civic friendship. Indeed, it is not clear that the
ideal was ever realized, for Greek history demonstrates
above all else an inability to form lasting political associations. Furthermore, the conditions under which
something like civic friendship might actually be realized are likely to be rare, and even if the ideal could be
achieved we may wish to ask whether it does not contain within itself a totalitarian temptation.

The ideal that Aristotle expresses—the political bond
as one of civic friendship—is to some extent belied by
the history of the polis. The ideal is what we today
might call a participatory-communal polity rather than a
liberal polity.[5] Friendship as we understand it today—
an intimate, personal, and private bond among a small
group of people—is for Aristotle only a more perfect
expression of the bond which unites the polis. The person becomes fully human, and fully free, only when
actively engaged in ruling and being ruled in turns.
Political activity, and the "positive freedom" which
such participation is said to bring, become necessary
constituents of a fully human existence. There is a qualitative difference—a moral difference perhaps—between

the liberal understanding of politics as activity necessary simply to leave the individual free for his or her private concerns, and the ideal of a participatory-communal polity: "the lively sense of oneself as a participant in a free state, concerned for the common good."⁶

It is widely believed, and often bemoaned, that this participatory ideal has been lost in political communities such as the United States. "In the modern state," Wilson Carey McWilliams writes, "civic fraternity is impossible and the best, or rather the safest, approximation of justice is procedural rather than substantive, limited to external conduct, and leaves the development of man's justly fearful spirit to others than the state."⁷ In such communities there is unlikely to be anything approximating civic friendship. McWilliams, with more than a touch of acidity, notes that "even the bar, which Duverger called 'the agora of modern democracies,' yields increasingly to the liquor cabinet."⁸ Nevertheless, whatever may be the truth about our society, it is probably misleading to judge it too quickly in the name of the Aristotelian ideal. For in reality the Greek city-states were torn by strife, some of it caused precisely by groups of friends.

Among Greek social institutions that of the *hetaery* was "among the strongest and most persistent, surviving numerous political and social revolutions and providing to its members a far closer and more intimate bond than was afforded by the Greek family."⁹ The *hetaery*—with roots in the Homeric age, but surviving through both aristocratic and democratic times into the Hellenistic period—was a permanent association of men of equal age and status. Although such friends were comrades-in-arms, the association of the *hetaery* was not formed solely for temporary aims or for achieving political goals. Festive gatherings and banquets were common among such friends. But politics was certainly important, and friends in such a group would engage jointly in warfare, litigation, and other forms of political activity (writing pamphlets, packing assemblies, giving bribes, voting as a unit, strategic interruptions of opponents' speeches). The result of such political activity by friends was certainly not to inculcate or strengthen an ideal of civic friendship. The opposite seems to have been the case. "It cannot be doubted that the deep divisions rending the Greek *polis* and the incessant enmities and party conflicts which prevented the Greeks from achieving a more lasting union were in part fuelled and reinforced by the institution of the *hetaery*."[10] Our tendency to romanticize Athens and the ideal of civic friendship may perhaps be checked if we remember that the Greek polis which more effectively managed to establish such a polity was Sparta, not Athens.[11] To see that is to begin to appreciate the political costs of civic friendship; for there is no guarantee that deep bonds of friendship can be readily domesticated within Aristotle's larger understanding of philia. And if they can, the cost to the human spirit may be great.

At the very least, it seems fair to say that an ideal like civic friendship could be approximated only under certain conditions, which are likely to be rare. It is not accidental that the polis was small or that a theorist like Rousseau, in articulating the ideal of a participatory-communal polity, should have argued for the necessity of smallness.[12] Michael Walzer, in discussing whether the citizen might have an obligation to live for the state (and not merely, occasionally, to die for it) has suggested some of the criteria which mark out associations which could be described as participatory-communal: "They are relatively small groups; they involve close, even intimate, relations; and they involve voluntary relations."[13] In short, polities of this sort begin to resemble a bond like personal friendship.

Considerations of size alone make civic friendship an unattainable ideal in many political communities today.

And theorists like McWilliams and Walzer view this as the chief failing of the modern state. If the political bond will not bear the moral weight which we give to a relation like friendship, it is sadly deficient and, perhaps, in need of "radical reconstruction."[14] What such theorists seek is a political community which does more than protect our right to pursue private purposes and goals that is, they seek something other than a liberal polity. They want a political community worth living for, to be a member of which involves a kind of moral transformation: from self-serving pursuit of private purposes to other-regarding service of the common good. And in the ideal of civic friendship or civic fraternity they find possibilities for such a transformation.

Such communities are, everyone is agreed, likely to be rare. Perhaps even that is too sanguine a forecast. The ideal of civic friendship is, I think, one which could not be fully realized; the cardinal political good of justice makes its realization impossible.[15] An example of a very simple political problem may make this clear. Let us suppose a community must distribute certain health-care benefits and in so doing must consider the claims of the following citizens. First, parents who want their young daughter to be permitted to spend another week recuperating in a hospital (where beds are short) rather than risk a too early return home. Second, a physician whose patient needs access to an expensive therapy. Third, a person whose friend has recently finished medical school and now wishes to begin his practice in a relatively affluent area where there is already a high ratio of doctors to patients. It does not seem morally wrong for the parents to seek extended hospitalization for their child, for the doctor to seek the scarce therapy for his patient, or for one friend to try to help another. Indeed, in at least the first two of these cases many people might think the parents and the doctor under a positive obligation to try to achieve these ends.

At the same time it must be granted that the particular states of affairs sought by any or all of these people may be incompatible with a genuinely just distribution of health-care benefits within the community. There is nothing wrong with these citizens seeking the particular goods they desire, and the various special relations in which they stand seem almost to require that they do so. Nevertheless, if theirs is to be or remain a community, they will require *public* authority which can direct citizens toward their common good. (And, of course, if theirs is a truly participatory-communal polity, the citizens may themselves—in assembly—constitute that public authority.) But the person or persons who constitute this public authority leave behind the particular goods they desire and become "the public reason and will, endowed with the power to direct private persons toward the common good."[16] They are no longer persons but public *personae*.

We see here the reason why civic friendship is an incoherent ideal. The fellow-citizen bond, precisely because it must concern itself with justice, is not a *personal* bond. The common good, even in such a simple political problem as that described above, is the object of no particular person's intention, not even that of the public persons in their private capacities. It is intended only by public *personae*. Nor should we be too quick to bemoan this. If human beings are as prone to sin as Christian belief suggests, it is probably important that political authority be impersonal. Personal authority in the political realm too easily becomes arbitrary and begins to approach the power of master over slave and, hence, to cease to be political altogether. Political authority, by uniting all citizens under an impersonal rule of law, makes justice its highest good. In so doing it abstracts from many factors which make our concrete personal histories unique, and it does this in order to protect against our sinful tendency to exclude our fellows from, rather than include them within, the scope of our affection and concern. In short, public authority must treat us impersonally in order to be fair. "When people are friends, they have no need of justice," Aristotle said. But that is unlikely to be true of any political community, however small, in a sinful world. And if it is not, then the ideal of civic friendship is unattainable. The truth rather—and the best we can or should hope for—is that justice in the political order should nourish and foster private friendships. That is not a self-regarding goal, even if it settles for something less universal than civic friendship; for private friendships, though not universal in scope, are genuinely other-regarding. It is important to complete Aristotle's sentence. "When people are friends, they have no need of justice, but when they are just, they need friendship in addition."

Thus far I have subjected the ideal of civic friendship to a threefold criticism. The very communities, such as the Greek city-state, in which the ideal was formulated demonstrate the instability of a political community conceived in such terms. Further, the conditions under which such an ideal could be realized are, even according to advocates of the ideal, very rare. (And indeed, since smallness of size is one of the necessary conditions, such a community would not really offer in very great measure the universality which personal friendships seem to lack.) And thirdly, the ideal is actually incoherent, since it conflicts with the necessary political good of justice and the impersonality which justice requires. Finally, I want to suggest, hesitantly but firmly, that a Christian ethic ought to recognize the ideal of civic friendship as essentially pagan, an example of inordinate and idolatrous love.

It is not hard to see why some people might find a new sense of meaning and purpose in a participatory-communal polity. In such a community one may have a sense of becoming a new person, a public person, and this qualitative change can be thought of as a kind of

moral transformation. It must be something like this
that Rousseau means by suggesting that our public life
is a life received from the community. As a member of a
people, he suggests, an individual is transformed "into
a part of a much greater whole, from which that same
individual will then receive, in a sense, his life and
being."[17] At least for the Christian thinker, such a
sentence should carry the scent of danger.

To say of the city-state, as Aristotle does in his *Politics* (I, ii), that it is the "final and perfect association"
which is "prior in the order of nature to the family and
the individual" too easily suggests that the most inclusive and self-sufficient of our groups should also
acquire moral primacy. Rousseau, the greatest modern
theorist of a participatory-communal polity, desired
exactly that, and in order to insure it, suggested as one
feature of a properly ordered polity a desiccated civil
religion. Recognizing certain political necessities, Rousseau also recognized certain Christian necessities—and
deplored them. With the coming of Christianity, he
wrote, "the state ceased to be a unity." And the consequence has been "an endless conflict of jurisdiction,
which has made any kind of good polity impossible in
Christian states, where men have never known whether
they ought to obey the civil ruler or the priest."[18] In
recognizing these Christian necessities Rousseau was
not mistaken.

Jesus of Nazareth, confessed by Christians to be the
promised one of God, was put to death by the political
powers of his day. That simple fact forced Christians
into a radical reevaluation—even demythologizing—of
political communities and their possibilities. Never
again for Christian thought could one be sure that the
good person and the good citizen would be identical,
that good ethics and good politics would necessarily
coincide. What Martin Hengel has called the "naive
unity" of religion and politics—but what in Rousseau is

far from naive—was disrupted forever in Christian thought. [19]

We do not receive our life and being, finally, from the political community. What we receive, or hope to receive, is some measure of justice and the freedom to seek elsewhere what politics cannot provide. A truly personal bond like friendship provides at least an intimation, even if a limited one, of the greater community which God is building; for friendship is a bond of love. Political community, by contrast, is impersonal and—however important for human life—cannot really extend the boundaries of *love.* That is no reason to denigrate its worth, but it is a reason, and a good one, not to seek from it more than it can give. In friendship and citizenship we have two different forms of human community which are not really analogous. Friendship involves love, genuine giving and receiving, but is limited in scope. The political bond, though more universal, is an impersonal bond of justice in the world of claim and counterclaim. Encountering a fellow-citizen is not like finding a friend.

This need not mean an exaltation of private bonds like friendship to the point where they always become more important than the political bond. That would be no better than the attempt to find in civic friendship what political community cannot—without becoming an idol—offer. Instead, what we should learn to say is that, if the forms of community are not analogous, there is no way to specify that one should always take priority over the other. There may be no way to stipulate in advance when one's obligations as a citizen take precedence over one's loyalties as a friend. But if my analysis is correct, it is surely possible that at least on some occasions we might rightly decide that a relation like friendship be given priority in our thought and action. *Moral* priority. This is not to ignore the broader relationships with distant neighbors. Indeed, it would

still be possible to say with Reinhold Niebuhr that the
free human spirit, in search of an ever-larger brotherhood, will always transcend the limits of natural communities.[20] However, that larger community, in order
to satisfy the human spirit, would have to extend the
boundaries of love, not the impersonal tie of the fellow-
citizen bond. Politics and ethics must always be distinguished. The comrade is not the friend.

II

There are, of course, forces other than Christian
belief which can—and in Western history did—shatter
the ideal of civic friendship. Among classical thinkers
there was one who, consciously rejecting what had
largely been common ground in antiquity, made no
place for civic friendship as an ideal. One of Epicurus's
"Principal Doctrines" reads: "Of the things that wisdom prepares for insuring lifelong happiness, by far
the greatest is the possession of friends." And, lest we
should be tempted to interpret this in terms of Aristotle's broader, civic understanding of philia, Epicurus
also taught: "When reasonable security from men has
been attained, then the security that comes from peace
of mind and withdrawal from the crowd is present,
sufficient in strength and most unmixed in well-being."[21]
Clearly, for Epicurus the value of political community
lay in the security it provided for private undertakings,
of which he thought friendship the most important and
fulfilling.

Epicurus seems to have been impressed by what we
may call the "spiritual" character of the friendship
bond.[22] Whereas the state is necessary for security and
mutual protection, and the family for the continuation
of the species, friendship cannot be said to be necessary
in so fundamental a way for the preservation of human
life. Rather it is necessary—here Epicurus certainly
agreed with other classical thinkers—for the *happy*

life. This "unnecessary" and "spiritual" character seemed to suggest that friendship was a higher, more meaningful relationship than the political or familial bonds. Naturally, however, this shift in viewpoint is not unrelated to political and social changes. That Epicurus should have come to regard friendship exclusively as a private rather than a civic bond may not be surprising, for the character of Greek political society was changing. Alexander the Great had intervened, and the age of empire was replacing the city-state. That is to say, Epicurus's world was probably one in which it would become increasingly difficult to imagine that philia could actually constitute a civic bond. The necessary criteria were no longer present, and the Epicurean Garden is a not unexpected withdrawal from a world in which politics no longer involves face-to-face encounters and ongoing dialogue.

In such a political world friendship may cease to be of political importance—a fact in which some, like Epicurus, will rejoice. But an Epicurean attitude of detachment is not the only reaction possible to such changed political circumstances. In becoming a purely private bond, philia need not cease to have political consequences of a certain sort. C. S. Lewis has written that "every real Friendship is a sort of secession, even a rebellion . . . , a pocket of potential resistance."[23] And that is the other possibility; private friendship may conflict with public goals or responsibilities. We can discern such a possibility in Cicero's *De Amicitia*.

The circumstances surrounding the assassination of Caesar provided the occasion for Cicero's treatise on friendship.[24] Cicero, like Caesar's assassins, had hoped that the Roman republic could be restored—a hope which foundered in face of the loyalty of Caesar's friends even after his death. And, indeed, the consequences for Cicero were personally disastrous. Marc Antony, Augustus, and Lepidus ordered his execution, principally because of his known friendship for Brutus, one of the

conspirators against Caesar. Moreover, Cicero's intimate friend Atticus (to whom *De Amicitia* is addressed)
had adopted publicly an Epicurean stance of political
indifference—thereby achieving a kind of security in
the midst of shifting political alignments. Atticus was,
for example, friend both to Cicero and Marc Antony
even after the latter had ordered Cicero's execution. It
is not surprising, therefore, that Cicero should have
taken the bond of friendship seriously, nor that he
should have discerned possibilities other than Epicurean withdrawal.

When friendship becomes private, it can become a
public threat. It can become, as Lewis put it, "a pocket
of potential resistance." The concerns and standards
one shares with one's friends may seem to override
public purposes and will strengthen an individual in
resisting public pressures. We are not surprised, therefore, to see Cicero discuss the question of "how far love
ought to go in friendship" (XI, 36). To this question
Cicero—never perhaps the most consistent thinker—
gives conflicting answers. The main line of his response,
it is fair to say, is summarized by him in the general rule
he several times enunciates: "Let this law be established
in friendship: neither ask dishonourable things, nor do
them, if asked. And dishonourable it certainly is, and not
to be allowed, for anyone to plead in defence of sins in
general and especially of those against the State, that
he committed them for the sake of a friend" (XII, 40).
Cicero tells the story—also recounted by Montaigne in
his own famous essay on friendship—of how the Roman
consuls, after condemning Tiberius Gracchus for stirring
up revolution against the republic, investigated all who
had been his friends. Among these was Gaius Blossius,
who offered as grounds for leniency his great friendship
for Tiberius Gracchus. Laelius, who was among those
examining him, asked Blossius whether he would have
done what Tiberius wished "even if he had requested
you to set fire to the Capitol?" The response was: "He

never would have requested me to do that, of course, but if he had I should have obeyed." And what appears to be Cicero's judgment is then expressed through the mouth of Laelius. "You see what an impious remark that was" (XI, 37).

Montaigne concluded otherwise. "Those who condemn his answer as seditious have no proper understanding of the problem. . . . A unique and dominant friendship dissolves all other obligations."[25] And Montaigne here only states firmly what E. M. Forster, in a famous remark, put slightly more tentatively.

> If I had to choose between betraying my country and betraying my friend I hope I should have the guts to betray my country. Such a choice may scandalize the modern reader. . . . It would not have shocked Dante, though. Dante places Brutus and Cassius in the lowest circle of Hell because they had chosen to betray their friend Julius Caesar rather than their country Rome.[26]

We can perhaps appreciate the compelling power of such a choice more clearly if we understand it as part of someone's story, not just as a stark, provocative pronouncement. Graham Greene's marvelous "spy story" *The Human Factor* provides such a story, for it is a profound depiction of the tension between personal loyalties and political bonds. It is the "human factor"— personal loyalty to his lover and wife Sarah, and to the Communist agent who had helped her escape South Africa—which leads Maurice Castle to become a spy. And when finally, after he appears to have been discovered, he tells Sarah the secret he has so long hidden from her, the reader is likely to sympathize at least partially with her reaction.

> "You haven't said a word of blame, Sarah."
> "What sort of word?"
> "Well, I'm what's generally called a traitor."
> "Who cares?" she said. She put her hand in his: it was an act more intimate than a kiss—one can kiss a stranger.

She said, "We have our own country. You and I and Sam. You've never betrayed that country, Maurice."[27]

As Castle had reflected to himself on one occasion, "A man in love walks through the world like an anarchist, carrying a time bomb."[28] Love can be dangerous, and once friendship becomes a private bond, the political consequences may be incalculable. Not all temperaments will be Epicurean. And, in fact, Cicero himself is not entirely of one mind on the question. On at least one occasion he qualifies his straightforward law of friendship. He suggests that

> if by some chance the wishes of a friend are not altogether honourable and require to be forwarded in matters which involve his life or reputation, we should turn aside from the straight path, provided, however, utter disgrace does not follow; for there are limits to the indulgence which can be allowed to friendship. (XVII, 61)

To which, the translator of the Loeb Classical Library edition of *De Amicita* adds in a footnote, "This is apparently at variance" with the view Cicero expressed earlier. Perhaps, however, this is an occasion when it is the mark of a serious intellect to countenance some inconsistency.

It is not clear that we should, or can, determine that the political bond must always take priority over the friendship bond, or *vice versa*. Those who emphasize a personal bond like friendship will of course be accused, in one of our barbaric neologisms, of "privatizing" life. But such an accusation should be rejected. To value one's friends is to find meaning and significance in a relationship with others, not simply in the self's goals and desires. This is not a rejection of the political world, but a new platform from which to view and evaluate it. Indeed, in its very detachment from the political realm friendship can, as we have seen, acquire new political significance; it can become revolutionary. Modern states understand this well.

The state always seeks to isolate its disobedient citizens, because it is far more likely to bend their wills to its own if it can break the cohesion of the group which initially planned the disobedience and convince its members that they are members no longer. But this only suggests that the men who run prisons are always very much aware of the sociology of disobedience.[29]

One need not, of course, paint so heroic and revolutionary a picture of the political significance of friendship. It is equally possible with Epicurus simply to adopt and maintain an attitude of detachment from politics—not because it is believed to be worthless, but because other goods are valued more highly. "The noble man is chiefly concerned with wisdom and friendship; of these, the former is a mortal good, the latter an immortal one."[30]

What is the case for disagreeing with such a view? Why might one think that Cicero was—the first time—correct to suggest that it was dishonorable for anyone "to plead in defence of sins . . . against the State, that he committed them for the sake of a friend?" In seeking to answer that question we will, I think, be driven back to the fact that the state is the largest, most self-sufficient and all-encompassing of our communities—driven back, that is, to Aristotle's view. Who could live without at least some measure of justice and some degree of order? Surely we must grant that political community, in providing these goods, brings to human life something more fundamental than friendship could ever give.

I see no reason to dispute this; indeed, we have already granted it in noting above the unnecessary or "spiritual" character of friendship. "It has no survival value; rather it is one of those things which give value to survival."[31] To grant the fact, however, is not to grant the conclusion drawn from it. Human beings are, I take it, interested not only in living but in living well—and if political community is necessary to live, friendship may be necessary to live well. We can understand the sense in which the goods political community provides are more fundamental; they are necessary for survival. But survival is not always—at least not for all of us—the highest good. The case for granting moral priority to the public, political bond rests largely on a tacit acceptance of survival as the highest good. Michael Walzer has expressed well the chief reason for doubting this case by noting that

> while the state may well provide or seek to provide goods for all its members, it is not clear that these add up to or include the highest good. Perhaps they are goods of the lowest common denominator and only for this reason available to all, for it may be that the highest good can be pursued only in small groups.[32]

If the claims of the political realm over against friendship cannot be definitively established on the basis of such a "lowest common denominator" notion of the good, we should not conclude that personal bonds like friendship can always claim priority either. No one who has taken seriously the active, other-regarding, and implicitly universal character of Christian love should be willing to grant that. Citizenship *is* a more universal bond; justice and order, even if goods of the lowest common denominator, *are* of inestimable importance for human life. It would be easy to let the "spiritual" nature of friendship deceive us into imagining that its claims always deserved priority. To do that, however, would be to forget the very mundane and unexciting needs of neighbors which Christian love seeks to serve. We do well to remember that the ideal of civic friendship in the polis was quite compatible with—probably dependent upon—a system of slavery. It may be that when some devote themselves to "living well" others may be forced to deal solely with the needs of survival. As Kierkegaard writes, "Even the person who is otherwise not inclined to praise God and Christianity does so when with a shudder he reflects on the dreadfulness in paganism of a caste system whereby . . . this ungodliness inhumanly teaches one man to disclaim relationship with another. . . ."[33] Agape will not despise lowest common denominator goods, for they are needed by every neighbor. There is wisdom in the observation of one of the greatest students of friendship that friendship betrays itself any time it frees itself from morality or enslaves itself to morality.[34]

In affirming the relative weight of the claims of politics we are not returning to the ideal of civic friendship. Rather, the attempt to foster justice can be understood as an attempt to insure for one's neighbors the opportunity to experience and enjoy personal ties of affection and attachment—ties such as friendship. If all are potential participants in that most intensely personal of relationships as children of one Father, and if our limited creaturely bonds of love are intimations of that greater community, then it is a worthwhile—even obligatory—endeavor to seek to help others have opportunity to pursue those intimations as best they can. This is, certainly, a chastened political ideal, far from the dreams of civic friendship and a participatory-communal polity. It is, in the best sense, a liberal ideal. We build cities—that is, engage in public life—in order to preserve private intimations of a greater community. Political life can be preserved from its totalitarian temptations and, at the same time, given its just due only when we are willing to hope for more than political communities can ever offer—to hope, in short, for a day when no one would call another person "citizen" or "comrade" but each would call the other "friend."

5. Friendship and Vocation

There is an apocryphal tale of the chronic absentee
colliery-worker who was asked by his exasperated
manager why he worked only four shifts every week,
"because," replied the man, "I can't live on three."
P. D. Anthony, *The Ideology of Work*

In order to commit ourselves to the well-being of our
neighbors, we do not necessarily have to become Fran-
ciscans. There is an important strand of Christian tradition which has believed that love can remain nonpreferential and yet be fitted for society through commitment to vocation. This has, in particular, been a Protestant ideal.[1] In our vocation we serve (some) neighbors
and find our place in a whole system of vocations used
by God to care for (many) neighbors.

There can be little doubt that the idea of vocation has
had enormous social and cultural significance. It suggests, in fact, an ideal of life very different from the
classical ideal in which persons found fulfillment and
were assured of their own worth through a life shared
with friends. By contrast, the idea of providence—when
taken seriously in Christian thought—has suggested
the related idea of the calling. God calls each of us to
some work in life and by his providential governance
uses our work to serve the needs of many neighbors.
The classical ideal remains particularistic and concerned,
to a large degree, with self-fulfillment. The Christian

ideal suggests a more universalistic emphasis and, at
least in its purer forms, seems to commend self-forget-
fulness in service of one's vocation.

These contrasting styles of life mark more than a
break between the two great cultures of the West,
however; they suggest possible choices for anyone at
any time. Boswell records that Dr. Johnson once said
of John Wesley, the great Methodist preacher who
logged thousands of miles on horseback while traveling
around England to preach,

> John Wesley's conversation is good, but he is never at
> leisure. He is always obliged to go at a certain hour. This
> is very disagreeable to a man who loves to fold his legs and
> have out his talk, as I do.

It would, in the whole of our cultural history, be hard to
find better paradigms of these two contrasting styles of
life. No one took more pleasure in conversation among
friends than Dr. Johnson. And few had a stronger
sense of vocation than John Wesley (referred to by one
biographer as "The Lord's Horseman"). And the tension between these two styles of life is noted in Dr.
Johnson's comment. Wesley's conversation is good,
but—driven as he is by the requirements of his calling
—he can never just sit down, fold his legs, and have out
his talk! Serious commitment to vocation means that
one lives to work, and we should not forget that it is
also possible to choose—as some have—to work to live,
while seeking delight and fulfillment in the bond of
friendship.

I

Although the concept of a calling as one's work in
life has been of great importance in Christian thought,
we could not say that it is particularly pronounced in
the Bible. The biblical writings concern themselves
more with God's calling of a people for himself or of a

person to exercise a special function for the good of this people. Thus, Israel—and the new Israel—is called as a people holy unto God, and Christians are given different gifts fitting them for various tasks within the body of Christ. It is, therefore, something genuinely new when St. Paul writes, "let every one lead the life which the Lord has assigned to him, and in which God has called him" (I Corinthians 7:17)—conflating the call to membership in God's people with the call to work of a certain sort. The impact of this passage, particularly in the hands of Luther and Calvin, was enormous. Of it Kenneth Kirk has written:

> The words 'call' and 'calling' here obviously have two meanings. There is the 'call' to be a Christian, and the 'calling' (as we say), or worldly avocation, already being followed when the call to Christianity comes. . . . Quite deliberately Paul places these secular conditions and circumstances—this profession in which a man happens to be at the time of his conversion—on the same spiritual level as that conversion itself. Each is a 'call' or 'calling' direct from God. . . . This 'Oriental,' this 'ascetic,' this Puritan who stands aloof from the everyday life of the world—it is to him we owe the great Christian truth that the most ordinary and secular employment can and should be regarded as a mission directly laid upon us by the Omnipotent God himself.[2]

It is true that this view did not always prevail within Christendom before the great Reformers articulated it with depth and power. Although Protestant polemic can sometimes overdo the contrast, medieval Catholicism did think of a vocation primarily as the call to the monastic life—which, of course, leaves the majority of Christians without a specifically religious vocation. One can truthfully say, therefore, with Einar Billing that

> the more fully a Catholic Christian develops his nature, the more he becomes a stranger to ordinary life, the more he departs from the men and women who move therein. But . . . the evangelical church does not seek to create

religious virtuosos, but holy and saintly men and women *in* the call.[3]

For the Reformers, at least in theory, every Christian becomes a monk—except that, now, the serious Christian life is lived out within the world, and the whole of that life is offered up to God.

It is common, since Weber explored the Protestant Ethic,[4] to note that Calvin's concept of the calling is more aggressive and disciplined than is Luther's. And though here again one could overdo the contrast, there is truth in this much of Weber's thesis. The Calvinist, if not Calvin himself, did want to master the world and reshape it to the glory of God. This task requires unresting activity and a disciplined life. Thus, as one author aptly puts it, "Puritans discovered a utopia of men without leisure."[5] We can see fairly clearly the ideas at work in the Protestant concept of the calling if we consider William Perkins's discussion.[6] Perkins, certainly a serious and judicious Puritan divine, may well have been the most important Puritan thinker in England at the beginning of the seventeenth century.

A vocation or calling is, Perkins writes, "*a certain kind of life, ordained and imposed on man by God, for the common good*" (p. 36). That is, in good scholastic fashion we can say that the efficient cause of one's calling is God and the final cause is the common or public good. Each of these is important for Perkins's discussion. A calling implies a Caller—that is, God. And Perkins uses two metaphors to relate God as efficient cause to the system of human callings: a military and a mechanical metaphor. In an army camp, Perkins notes, the general appoints each man to his particular place, in which he is to remain against the enemy. And if each man fulfills his appointed task faithfully, the army will function well. Even so, Perkins suggests, "it is in humane societies: God the Generall, appointing to every man his particular calling . . ." (p. 37). (It is worth noting in passing that, while military modes of organi-

zation may often be necessary in human life, few of us regard it as the most desirable way to live. Such organization may value insufficiently the distinctive characteristics of different persons.)
Perkins's other metaphor is mechanical. "Againe, in a clocke, made by the art and handy-worke of man, there be many wheeles, and every one hath his severall motion, some turne this way, some that way, some goe softly, some apace: and they are all ordered by the motion of the watch" (p. 37). And Perkins finds a "notable resemblance" between this and the way in which God, in his special providence, allots to every person a particular calling. Well-oiled parts of a mechanism—that, it is not unfair to say, is what human beings become in such a system of vocations.

So much for the efficient cause. What of the final cause of our callings? The end of this system of vocations is the common good. Service in one's calling, if undertaken seriously and faithfully, will benefit others. One can be confident of that because God—the great General or, as we prefer, Clockmaker—has so arranged the system of callings with the welfare of humanity at heart. We could, of course, interpret this in a kind of *laissez-faire* manner: Everyone tends to his own knitting and God, like an invisible hand, sees to it that the system of callings fits together. But Perkins does not intend us to think of vocations in that way. Indeed, he explicitly rejects as wicked "that common saying, *Every man for himselfe, and God for us all*" (p. 39). We are to look, in our callings, not to our own interests but to the common good. It is, of course, true that God could care for human beings simply through an immediate exercise of his power, but he chooses to work mediately. He chooses "that men should be his instruments, for the good of one another" (p. 56). It is in service of this end that we "joyne . . . our callings together" (p. 56). What we see very clearly here is the universalistic impulse built into this Christian understanding of vocation. Though any individual's vocation will, of course, be limited in focus, the system of callings as a whole—under the providential governance of God—serves the needs of many neighbors.

It is this universalistic impulse which permits a system of vocations to place our works of love in a more universally other regarding context while still allowing special attachment to certain tasks and to needs of certain people. But again, this is not to suggest that individuals can settle contentedly into their routine tasks, assuming that God will care for distant neighbors. Einar Billing has suggested that "the call constantly has to struggle against two adversaries: stereotyped workmanship and unresponsible idealism."[7] On the one hand, the person called by God must rigorously restrict his efforts to the actual task appointed by God. If this is not done, no one's needs are really served. At the same time, however, one must remain open to possibilities for "an infinite expansion of our work." God's call may, after all, lead in new directions, and "we must be prepared for each new assignment he may have for us."[8] Thus, the universalistic impulse has a place directly within the life of each individual called; its place lies in the openness to possibilities for infinite expansion. But that is, I think, only a qualification, even if an important one. Universality is, in the main, a feature not of any particular vocation but of the whole system of vocations.

The consequences of this understanding of vocation are of great significance. To begin with, work is elevated to a central place in life. It is serious business, since, after all, we are called to our work by God and used by him to serve the needs of our fellows. Perkins, for example, makes this point at great length. The chief enemies of the calling are idleness and sloth, which Perkins, in all the seriousness with which an earlier age could invest such terms, calls "damnable sinnes" (p. 42). Indeed, to make his point Perkins uses a scriptural reference which was a Puritan favorite: "The servant that had received but one talent, is called an evillservant, because he was slouthfull in the use of it" (p. 43). We need only remember John Wesley, a man never at leisure to have out his talk, to understand what serious business a vocation could become. Such a calling leaves little place for self-indulgence within life. We may simply note, without in any way suggesting that folding one's legs and having out one's talk is unworthy, that wholehearted commitment to our calling may leave little time for such pleasures. The inevitable result is that deep personal relationships like friendship, without precisely being denigrated, become harder and harder to sustain. They are not so much criticized as they are squeezed out of life. Personal significance is found in one's calling—or it is not found at all.

Not only is little place left in life for the apparent self-indulgence of a bond like friendship, but something begins to happen to the work one does, as well. Whatever inadequacies Weber's thesis may contain, it is not hard to see with him that the idea of a system of callings is related to the idea of division of labor.[9] At the same time that the worker is called upon to find personal significance in his work—it is, after all, God's call—the work itself becomes increasingly impersonal and subject to rational economic calculation. The worker is a soldier in the great army of which God is General, or a part in the machine constructed by God the Clockmaker. Each person should carry out faithfully and seriously his or her function in the system of callings. And one's place in that system is determined not by personal bonds like friendship but by considerations of efficiency and fairness. Devotion to the task at hand becomes of supreme importance.

Quite often, perhaps because we prefer not to think about it, we do not appreciate what commitment to a vocation really requires, how much like an overriding religious commitment it can be. Dorothy Sayers has illustrated this point brilliantly in *Gaudy Night*.[10] The mystery which needs solving in this story results from a case of academic dishonesty. Sayers's plot revolves around a women's college at Oxford—a college which is suddenly subjected to various attacks on property and persons. The attacks, it is finally discovered, have been made by Annie, who works at the college. Years before these events Annie's husband had been driven from academic life because Miss de Vine—now teaching at Shrewsbury College where Annie works—discovered that he had suppressed evidence which would have disproven his thesis. Interestingly, one of Annie's acts of violence involved defacing a novel called *The Search* "at the exact point where the author upholds, or appears for the moment to uphold, the doctrine that loyalty to the abstract truth must over-ride all personal considerations" (p. 360). And it was, of course, precisely such commitment to the truth, understood as integral to her vocation, which had led Miss de Vine to expose Annie's husband. At one point in the story Miss de Vine, talking with Harriet, discusses her own view of what vocational commitment requires. She and Harriet agree that if we find a subject in which we're content with second-rate work, that cannot be where our commitment really lies.

> "No," said Miss de Vine. "If you are once sure what you do want, you find that everything else goes down before it like grass under a roller—all other interests, your own and other people's. Miss Lydgate wouldn't like my saying that, but it's as true of her as of anybody else. She's the kindest soul in the world, in things she's indifferent about, like the peculations of Jukes. But she hasn't the slightest mercy on the prosodical theories of Mr. Elkbottom. She wouldn't countenance those to save Mr. Elkbottom from hanging. She'd say she couldn't. And she couldn't, of course. If she actually *saw* Mr. Elkbottom writhing in humiliation, she'd be sorry, but she wouldn't alter a paragraph. That would be treason. One can't be pitiful where one's own job is

concerned. You'd lie cheerfully, I expect, about anything except—what?"

"Oh, anything!" said Harriet, laughing, "Except saying that somebody's beastly book is good when it isn't. I can't do that. It makes me a lot of enemies, but I can't do it."

"No, one can't," said Miss de Vine. "However painful it is, there's always one thing one has to deal with sincerely, if there's any root to one's mind at all. I ought to know, from my own experience. Of course, the one thing may be an emotional thing; I don't say it mayn't. One may commit all the sins in the calendar, and still be faithful and honest towards one person. If so, then that one person is probably one's appointed job. I'm not despising that kind of loyalty; it doesn't happen to be mine, that is all." (P. 150).

Clearly, Miss de Vine is a woman who knows what an overriding vocational commitment means and the way in which it may make purely personal concerns secondary. One must simply get on with the job—and getting on with it may leave no room even for pity, much less for friendship. Miss de Vine does grant that this kind of commitment might be given not to a vocation but to another person (as Annie gave it to her husband). She does not, she says, despise that kind of personal loyalty. Harriet presses the point.

"Then you're all for the impersonal job?"
"I am," said Miss de Vine.
"But you say you don't despise those who make some other person their job?"
"Far from despising them," said Miss de Vine, "I think they are dangerous." (P. 151)

In the context of the story her words are prophetic, since Annie—whose overriding commitment is one of loyalty to a person—is indeed dangerous. More to the point, though, such persons are dangerous because their commitment is so partial, so preferential. Commitment to a vocation is not like that. The vocation serves many people's needs; God sees to that. But the worker himself shows no particular preference; his commitment is to the work. Miss de Vine is, I think, correct to suggest that such commitment may be less dangerous than Annie's. But it exacts a price, and Harriet is not mistaken to suggest that it is "impersonal." Humanity has been greatly enriched by the Protestant concept of a system of callings in which each finds his or her place. Whether individual lives have been enriched by it is another, and harder, question.

II

"Dead matter leaves the factory ennobled and transformed, where men are corrupted and degraded," wrote Pius XI.[11] And it may be that the Christian concept of vocation has fostered that corruption; at the very least, it can certainly obscure it. We noted above that the concept of the calling could invest work with the dimension of personal significance while at the same time turning work into an impersonal task and possibly (as a result of division of labor) a mindless task. In such circumstances, the affirmation that we can find personal significance in our work begins to sound a bit shrill—as if, just possibly, we were trying to convince ourselves.

To regard work as a calling is to suggest that we live to work, that our work is of central significance for our person. Still more, the calling gives to work a religious significance which it is not likely to acquire in any other way. Thus, Dorothy Sayers could suggest that work expresses something essential in human nature; for it is a natural function of human beings who are made in the image of their Creator. The worker gives full expression to an essential feature of our shared human nature. "His satisfaction comes, in the godlike manner, from looking upon what He has made and finding it very good."[12] Sayers was no fool, of course, and she realized that it is not easy to say this about the work many, probably most, people spend their lives doing. But to realize that, and nevertheless keep on emphasizing the significance of work, is to risk obscuring something important. For the Greeks, friendship was clearly important for self-fulfillment. "No one," writes Aristotle, "would choose to live without friends, even if he had all other goods."[13] In coming to know the friend as "another self," one came to know oneself as well and acquired a sense of one's personal significance. To suggest that we live to work—and to cloak this in the religious garb of the calling—is to try to have work play a similar role in our lives. It is to make work as central in our sense of who we are as friendship was for the Greeks.

It is crucial to see that when we take this step we have really distorted the significance of the calling as it was understood and developed by early Protestants like Perkins. The point of the calling was, quite simply, that it was appointed by God to serve neighbors. If along the way some self-fulfillment came as well, there was nothing wrong with that, but it was hardly the point of the calling. Our modern notion—into which even so independent a thinker as Sayers could be lured —that the point of work is to give meaning, purpose, and fulfillment to life is a degradation of the calling. It is a degradation against which we should have been guarded by both our experience and our theological tradition.

Our experience should surely have taught us that, although some people seem to find their work satisfying in itself, it is equally true that "work, for most people, has always been ugly, crippling, and dangerous."[14] We may in good conscience recommend such work as service to the neighbor or even as an instrument of spiritual discipline, but it ought be cloaked in no other religious garb. When the system of vocations as we experience it today is described in terms which make work the locus of self-fulfillment, Christian ethics ought to object—on the empirical ground that this is far from true, and on the theological ground that vocation ought not make self-fulfillment central. When work as we know it emerges as the dominant idea in our lives—when we identify ourselves to others in terms of what we do for a living, work for which we are paid—and when we glorify such work in terms of self-fulfillment, it is time for Christian ethics to speak a good word for working simply in order to live. Perhaps we need to suggest today that it is quite permissible, even appropriate, simply to work in order to live and to seek one's fulfillment elsewhere—in personal bonds like friendship, for example.

Such a suggestion is likely to meet with disapproval from every side, and this disapproval is likely to use that magic word "alienation." Put most simply, "alienation means that the worker has little sense of personal investment in his or her work. We work at one thing—live for another. The alienated worker, we are told, understands his work only instrumentally—as a means to having the wherewithal and the opportunity to pursue other ends and values. And, the argument continues, such an alienated worker—one who works only to live—can scarcely live a fully human existence. Self-fulfillment is impossible in such circumstances. We are by now so accustomed to taking this purported fact of alienation for granted that it comes as something of a shock to be told, as P. D. Anthony has recently argued, that "man can be regarded as alienated from his work only when he has been subjected to an ideology which requires him to be devoted to it."[15] Yet, Anthony is quite correct. Alienation becomes possible only when, first, work has been given central place in human life, and, second, it is assumed that we are to gain a sense of personal fulfillment from our work. The idea of the calling contributed to the first of these; degradation of that idea to the second. The end of this road becomes apparent in Marxist thought, where alienation has been such a central concept. According to Marx, human beings "begin to distinguish themselves from animals as soon as they begin to *produce* their means of subsistence."[16] The human being is a worker—and once that is made central, alienation becomes a possibility, indeed, a likelihood. As the place and importance of work in human life are exaggerated, the undesirable characteristics of work become more glaring and objectionable. It is possible to be alienated from our work only if we first imagine that we were to find in it a high degree of personal fulfillment. Whatever its defects, it is one of the virtues of capitalism that it must allow people simply to work for money and seek fulfillment elsewhere. Indeed, we might say with Anthony that "capitalism represents an imperfect stage in development towards the absolute transcendency of economic values and an associated ideology of work, the fullest development of which is represented in Marxism."[17]

If our experience should have warned us against making work an essential feature of human nature and the locus of self-fulfillment, so ought our theological tradition. I have already noted that the idea of the calling, in its pure form, had little to do with achieving personal fulfillment. For Luther and Calvin one worked in order not to become a burden to others and because God had appointed for one this particular calling as service to one's neighbors. Even with those qualifications, however, it remains true that the calling may have given work greater centrality in life than it should have, and it is not surprising that coupled with exhortations to faithfulness in one's calling were vigorous attacks on idleness and begging. And in the modern world, work has certainly begun to have the status of an idol. In such circumstances we need to reassert other aspects of our theological tradition. Karl Barth, arguing that human beings, for the most part, work to live rather than live to work, directed a much needed polemic against the idol of work.

It is of a piece with the rather feverish modern over-
estimation of work and of the process of production that
particularly at the climax of the 19th century, and even
more so in our own, it should be thought essential to man,
or more precisely to the true nature of man, to have a vocation in this sense. On such a view it is forgotten that there
are children and the sick and elderly and others for whom
vocation in this sense can be only the object either of
expectation and preparation or of recollection. It is also
forgotten that there are the unemployed, though these are
certainly not without a vocation. Finally, it is forgotten
that there are innumerable active women who do not have
this kind of vocation.[18]

It is worth recalling that it was possible for biblical
writers to speak of the promise of God for his people
as *rest*. "So then, there remains a sabbath rest for the
people of God; for whoever enters God's rest also ceases
from his labors as God did from his" (Hebrews 4:9f.).
And, indeed, that sabbath rest, as it even now recurs in
the weekly cycle of Christian life, is already testimony
to the fact that work offers no final fulfillment for human existence.

This is what we ought to have learned and what
Christian ethics should call to mind: that work is not an
essential feature of a human life, that the point of work
is not our own fulfillment but service to others, that
work has its limits and need not always make it impossible for us to fold our legs and have out our talk. The
proper tone—which does not idolize work but which
grants its necessity—was captured quite well by Calvin
when he wrote of the calling: "each man will bear and
swallow the discomforts, vexations, weariness, and
anxieties in his way of life, when he has been persuaded
that the burden was laid upon him by God."[19]

III

The Christian concept of vocation becomes degraded
whenever it is seen primarily as a source of self-fulfill-

ment. In a world which thinks of work in that way there would seem to be good reason to prefer the bond of friendship to work; for, though the self is fulfilled in friendship, the bond is reciprocal, and others are truly loved for their own sakes. And even if work is understood properly and the calling seen only as a God-appointed means of serving the neighbor, there should be limits to what the calling can ask of us. Even if a system of callings has a universalistic impulse, the final responsibility for meeting those universal needs rests with God, who structures this system of callings. Faithfulness in our vocation, even faithfulness which is sensitive to the danger of "stereotyped workmanship" and alert to the possibilities for "infinite expansion" of the task, does not mean unlimited responsibility. The calling is a way of recognizing the legitimate claims of distant neighbors without imagining that any of us is responsible for meeting all of them and without driving out of life any place for special, preferential bonds of love like friendship. In this way, and unlike the Franciscan love which breaks through all normal bonds of life, the concept of the calling makes it possible for love to be universal yet "fitted for society."

We should not imagine, however, that the fit can ever be perfect—that the claims of friendship and the claims of vocation can be perfectly reconciled in this life. There are several reasons why this is not possible, some grounded in sociological observations about modern Western societies, others grounded more deeply in the structure of Christian theology. Even if our affirmation of vocation is a chastened one and our appreciation of the place of friendship cautious, we will find that a life which does justice to the claims of each is not easy to live.

A world in which vocation has become central must be a world in which preferential bonds like friendship become increasingly remote from large stretches of our life. We do not hire and fire people on the basis of friendship; indeed, to do so strikes many of us as more than a little suspect. Thus, in the world of vocation as in that of politics, we purchase fairness at the price of impersonality. Further, as Miss de Vine realized, serious commitment to a vocation may leave little time for personal concerns; the task has its own built-in necessities and momentum. More important still may be the fact that many vocations in our world require mobility. We may have to move at any time. And certainly any advancement in our work—advancement which may well put us in a position to serve more neighbors—will often require change of location. The result is predictable. "Deep personal bonds are discouraged by the knowledge of transcience," and we learn to keep our commitments tentative and provisional.[20] One does not have to be concerned primarily with personal advancement to be affected in this way. We need only be seriously committed to our God-appointed task and open to the possibilities for "infinite expansion" of that task. The circle soon becomes a vicious one; for those who are enticed by vocational necessities to keep their personal commitments tentative become increasingly isolated and increasingly tempted to try to "live to work." In such a world, as William May has perceptively noted, "the Bell Telephone Company and the Hallmark card industry grow rich on the conscience of Americans uneasy about their overextended personal loyalties."[21]

Thus, the tension between the claims of vocation and friendship is partly a result of certain characteristics of a society like ours, one which has been organized increasingly around the hub of vocation. But the roots of the difficulty go considerably deeper. We may discern this in a paradox which St. Anselm saw in the divine will.[22] Anselm distinguished a divine *disposition* from a divine *distribution*. The divine disposition requires that we go where God wills, that we be obedient to his disposition, even if it should require separation from friends. At the same time, however, the divine distribution bestows the gift of friendship in our lives. This paradox, which Anselm finds in his own experience, is one of the central problems of the Christian life. Earthly affections like friendship are bestowed by the Creator and no fully human life can do without them; yet that same God may lay upon us a task which makes the enjoyment of such attachments difficult or impossible. "The cause of God," Adele Fiske writes, "may often run contrary to human affection. . . . Anselm says rather piteously: 'do not love me less because God does his will in me.'"

God gives both the earthly bond of friendship, which enriches life, and the calling, which serves the neighbor. Theories which rest content in preferential loves or, alternatively, which glorify the calling above all else fail to appreciate the paradox of the divine will which Anselm discerned. The tension between bonds of particular love and a love which is open to every neighbor (in the calling) cannot be overcome by any theory, however intricate. Our thinking can only warn against certain mistakes, certain wrong turnings which we might take. But this central problem of the Christian life must be lived, not just thought. This much, if Adele Fiske is correct, Anselm clearly realized. "St. Anselm soberly faces the fact that God's will often seems to work against itself, destroying the gift it has given. This problem is solved *ambulando,* or it is not solved; he suffers and admits it, but does not try to escape by turning away from human love to love 'God alone'." The tension between particular bonds and a more universally open love—of which the tension between friendship and vocation is an instance—cannot be eliminated for creatures whose lives are marked by the particularities of time and place but who yet are made to share with all others the praise of God. The tension between particular and universal love is "solved" only as it is lived out in a life understood as pilgrimage toward the God who gives both the friend and the neighbor.

If Christian commitment to vocation shattered forever the classical ideal of a unified life devoted to
leisured conversation with friends and contemplation,
this was not without loss. And Christian thought at its
best has never pretended that vocation exacted no price.
Only the glorification of vocation as self-fulfillment,
which is simultaneously a degradation of the true concept of the calling, has led us to believe that no price
was asked. We have, in a sense, sought once again to
unify life. As the Greek found a unified life centered in
friendship, so the modern pagan seeks it in vocation.
But a proper Christian understanding will forego that
unity in favor of a life which, recognizing that God gives
both the friend and the neighbor, prefers to face the
problem *ambulando*. It may be wise to allow the final
word about friendship and vocation to St. Augustine,
who, as much as anyone, shattered that classical ideal
of a unified life. In Book XIX of his *City of God* Augustine considers whether the best life is one of leisure
(and contemplation) or one of action—or some combina-
tion of these. After making all the appropriate qualifications—that one should not be so active as to have no
need or time for God, that the active life is not to be
sought for reasons of ambition—Augustine comes to
terms with the life he himself would have loved, a life
of leisured pursuit of truth among friends, and the life
he actually lived as a bishop.

> We see then that it is love of truth that looks for sanctified
> leisure, while it is the compulsion of love that undertakes
> righteous engagement in affairs. If this latter burden is
> not imposed on us, we should employ our freedom from
> business in the quest for truth and its contemplation, while
> if it is laid upon us, it is to be undertaken because of the
> compulsion of love. Yet even in this case the delight in
> truth should not be utterly abandoned, for fear that we
> should lose this enjoyment and that compulsion should
> overwhelm us.[23]

EPILOGUE

We had occasion to note earlier that friendship has a kind of "spiritual" character. It is not necessary for survival, even if it is important for living well. It is not biologically necessary for the continuance of the species in the way kinship or marriage might be said to be. Reflection upon this fact might lead us to exalt highly the importance of the bond of friendship within human life, especially when contrasted with other special bonds which have their origin in biological necessity. Thus, Montaigne could write of the bond between parents and children:

> There have been philosophers—witness Aristippus—who have disdained this natural tie. When someone insisted on the affection that he owed his children, since they came out of him, he began to spit, saying that this comes out of him too, and that we also breed lice and worms. And there was that other whom Plutarch tried to reconcile with his brother. "I do not value him any more highly," he said, "for having come out of the same hole."[1]

And with such sentiments Montaigne had some sympathy!

At the conclusion of a discussion designed, to some extent, to make place for friendship within Christian thought, it may be well to remind ourselves that within this theological tradition marriage has been paid more heed than friendship. And however much one may wish to rehabilitate friendship, this fact should give us pause. Perhaps friendship is too "spiritual" to be entirely safe.[2]

104

It is interesting to set side by side the description of friendship as "one soul in bodies twain" with the Christian understanding of marriage as a "one flesh" union (two souls in one body). The union which marriage fosters and nourishes is fleshly—a sharing which is not allowed to forget the importance of earthly, historical life. And the child, as the natural fruit of the marital union, is an ever present reminder that this union must turn outward, that it cannot rest in contented exclusivity. Such a fleshly bond is, perhaps, a better reminder than friendship that we dare not transcend too quickly the burdens of earthly life—burdens of fidelity, politics, and vocation. For it is in taking seriously such burdens that we encounter the neighbor who has been given us.

But the friend is also given us. Whatever its dangers, friendship is surely a bond of great significance for human life. No adequate theological ethic can fail to make place for it. When Christ came into this world, he came to his own, John's Gospel tells us. And the divine love which Christ displays—God's agape—cannot therefore be entirely alien to the needs and possibilities of our human nature. At the same time, it was—or so Christian thought would have it—essential that Christ come; for there were in the divine agape he displayed possibilities beyond those of our nature. To say this is to state the limits within which theological ethics must consider the love of friendship. We must affirm friendship and value its place in human life, not just grant it grudging acceptance in a system which really has no place for it. At the same time we must never fail to note friendship's own limits, against which agape strains. We cannot without destroying our humanity turn from the love of friendship and deny it an important place in human life. Neither can we simply rest content in a partial, particular love like friendship; that too would be a denial of our humanity. If we rest content in friendship we will fail to see both its source and destination in God. And in failing to see that, we will fail to see friendship for what it is, and we will remove it from the only environment in which it can, finally, flourish.

If this provides no fully satisfactory resolution of the tension between philia and agape, the reader is reminded that none was promised! That tension is not to be transcended in thought but to be experienced and lived. We return in the end to the image of the Christian life as pilgrimage. If in the course of that sojourn friendship with its delights may often constitute a pleasant resting place, we ought never to mistake it for home. That, of course would be to miss the point.

Notes

Prologue

1. Jeremy Taylor, "Discourse on the Nature and Offices of Friendship," vol. I of *Works,* ed. by R. Heber, rev. and corrected by C. P. Eden (London, 1847), p. 72.

2. Several Greek and Latin words will be used so often in the pages that follow that it would prove a mere distraction to italicize them at every occurrence. Hereafter, therefore, the following will be printed as if they were ordinary English words: agape, philia, eros, caritas, and polis.

3. Adolf Harnack, Excursus I: "Friends," in *The Mission and Expansion of Christianity* (New York: Harper Torchbooks, 1962), p. 421. Harnack says that the use of "friends of God" as a self-designation is derived from a reference to Abraham as "friend of God" (cf., Isaiah 41:8 and James 2:23).

1. *Friendship as a Preferential Love*

1. Søren Kierkegaard, *Works of Love,* trans. Howard and Edna Hong (New York: Harper Torchbooks, 1964), p. 70.

2. See Horst H. Hutter, "Friendship in Theory and Practice: A Study of Greek and Roman Theories of Friendship in Their Social Settings" (Ph.D. diss., Stanford University, 1972).

3. My interpretation of the *Phaedrus* has been informed by Josef Pieper, *Enthusiasm and Divine Madness,* trans. Richard and Clara Winston (New York: Harcourt, Brace & World, 1964). All citations of *Phaedrus* in the text will be taken from the translation of W. C. Helmbold and W. G. Rabinowitz (Indianapolis: Bobbs-Merrill, 1956).

4. The social context presupposed is, of course, that of upper-class Athenian society of the sixth to fourth centuries B.C., in which pederasty was widespread. For a thorough discussion of this social context, see K. J. Dover, *Greek Homosexuality* (Cambridge, Mass.: Harvard University Press, 1978).

5. Plato, *Symposium*, trans. Michael Joyce, in *The Collected Dialogues of Plato,* ed. Edith Hamilton and Huntington Cairns (New York: Bollingen Foundation, 1961).

6. Aristotle, *Nicomachean Ethics,* trans. Martin Ostwald (Indianapolis: Bobbs-Merrill, 1962). All citations in the text are from this translation.

7. See John M. Cooper, "Aristotle on the Forms of Friendship," *The Review of Metaphysics* 30 (June 1977), 618–648. Cooper suggests, quite helpfully, that we call these three forms of friendship (1) advantage-friendship, (2) pleasure-friendship, and (3) character-friendship. This makes clear that Aristotle's friendship based on the good is an attachment to (and choice of) the character of the one who is loved.

8. William F. May, "The Sin Against the Friend: Betrayal," *Cross Currents* 17 (1967).

9. Hutter, pp. 100f.

10. St. Augustine, *Confessions,* trans. Rex Warner (New York: New American Library, 1963). All citations in the text are from this translation.

11. Marie Aquinas McNamara, *Friendship in Saint Augustine* (Fribourg: The University Press, 1958), p. 221.

12. St. Augustine, *On Christian Doctrine,* Nicene and Post-Nicene Fathers, First Series, vol. II (New York: Scribners, 1908).

13. Adele M. Fiske, *Friends and Friendship in the Monastic Tradition* (Cuernavaca, Mexico: Centro Intercultural de Documentacion, 1970), p. 2/3.

14. For a clear summary discussion of these different directions of movement see Gene Outka, *Agape: An Ethical Analysis* (New Haven and London: Yale University Press, 1972), pp. 268–274.

15. Jonathan Edwards, *The Nature of True Virtue* (Ann Arbor: University of Michigan Press, 1960), p. 5.

16. Ibid., p. 86.

17. Josef Pieper, *About Love,* trans. Richard and Clara Winston (Chicago: Franciscan Herald Press, 1974), p. 51.

18. Jeremy Taylor, "Discourse on the Nature and Offices of Friendship," vol. I of *Works,* ed. by R. Heber, rev. and corrected by C. P. Eden (London, 1847). Page references will be given within parentheses in the body of the text.

19. Kierkegaard, p. 63.

20. Ibid., pp. 64f.

21. Ibid., p. 65.

22. I would not pretend that this is a complete treatment of Kierkegaard's richly puzzling *Works of Love,* though it is adequate as far as it goes. One might suggest that Kierkegaard represents none of the positions I have explored. He neither "builds up" from particular attachments to universal love nor "builds down" from Christian love to particular loves. Instead, having "teleologically suspended" the universal, he calls for love of neighbor—though, of course, that may mean any neighbor or all neighbors one by one. One loves each neighbor in all his or her particularity, but loves nonpreferentially. I must confess, however, that I have never been able to understand how such neighbor-love could incorporate into its commitment any elements of philia or eros. The essential Kierkegaard seems to me to be the one who uproots all preferential loves. If that is correct, he eliminates rather than solves the problem with which this chapter deals.

23. See Outka, p. 270.

24. Joseph Butler, Dissertation "On the Nature of Virtue," appended to *The Analogy of Religion Natural and Revealed,* Morley's Universal Library edition (London: George Routledge & Sons, 1884), p. 301 (emphasis added). In short, though creatures must be deontologists, God may perhaps be a rule utilitarian.

25. For an interesting attempt to make this fact central to an understanding of the moral life, though an example that, to my mind, is marred by the central place given self-realization, see Germain Grisez and Russell Shaw, *Beyond the New Morality: The Responsibilities of Freedom* (Notre Dame and London: University of Notre Dame Press, 1974).

26. Butler, p. 302.

27. Reinhold Niebuhr, *The Children of Light and the Children of Darkness* (New York: Charles Scribner's Sons, 1944), p. 83.

28. Daniel Day Williams, *The Spirit and The Forms of Love* (New York and Evanston: Harper & Row, 1968), p. 3.

29. Cf. Williams, pp. 67ff. and Outka, pp. 24ff.

30. Reinhold Niebuhr, *The Nature and Destiny of Man,* vol. II: *Human Destiny* (New York: Charles Scribner's Sons, 1964), p. 72. I am not suggesting that Niebuhr fits what Williams calls the "Franciscan type"; indeed, Williams himself puts Niebuhr into a different category (his "Evangelical type"). This is largely, however, because Niebuhr does not think that within history such an agapeic life can actually be lived fully. It could be lived only when our own interests and desires and no one else's are at stake—a rare occurrence indeed. Niebuhr is even willing to say that many Christian actions need not, therefore, conform to the ideal of agape but must instead conform to the norms of relative justice and mutual love (p. 88).

31. Jack T. Sanders, *Ethics in the New Testament: Change and Development* (Philadelphia: Fortress Press, 1975), p. 8.

32. Kierkegaard, p. 97.

2. *Friendship as a Reciprocal Love*

1. Plato, *Lysis,* trans. J. Wright in *The Collected Dialogues of Plato,* ed. Edith Hamilton and Huntington Cairns (New York: Bollingen Foundation, 1961).

2. It is possible to argue that friendship is not really as self-centered as my "stark contrast" may suggest. See, for example, John M. Cooper, "Aristotle on the Forms of Friendship " *The Review of Metaphysics* 30 (June 1977), 618–648. Cooper suggests that even pleasure-friendship and advantage-friendship should be understood retrospectively rather than prospectively. That is, I may wish someone well because I recognize him as one from whom I have received pleasure or advantage, and thus I may come to wish him well independently of whether I receive reciprocal advantage or pleasure (p. 634). Yet, even Cooper grants that this disinterested goodwill remains within the context of an association motivated primarily by self-seeking and, hence, the ethical problem posed by reciprocity remains. Furthermore, this problem exists even with respect to Aristotle's highest form of friendship, which Cooper calls character-friendship. Aristotle makes clear that the man of good moral character, though he may make great sacrifices for his friends and be far from what most people call an egoist, will still be careful always to

assign the greatest good—nobility—to himself (IX, 8). Also worth consulting is another article by Cooper: "Friendship and the Good in Aristotle," *The Philosophical Review* 86 (July 1977), 290–315.

3. Seneca, *Ad Lucilium: Epistulae Morales I*, trans. Richard M. Gummere, Loeb Classical Library (London: William Heinemann, 1925), pp. 42–57. All citations in the text are taken from this translation of Epistle IX.

4. Epicurus, *Letters, Principal Doctrines, and Vatican Sayings*, trans. Russel M. Geer, Library of Liberal Arts (Indianapolis: Bobbs-Merrill, 1964), Vatican Saying XXIII, p. 67.

5. C. S. Lewis, *The Four Loves* (New York: Harcourt Brace Jovanovich, 1960), p. 169.

6. Søren Kierkegaard, *Works of Love*, trans. Howard and Edna Hong (New York: Harper Torchbooks, 1964), p. 227. Future citations of *Works of Love* will be given in the body of the text by page number within parentheses.

7. Josef Pieper, *About Love*, trans. Richard and Clara Winston (Chicago: Franciscan Herald Press, 1974), p. 90.

8. S.T., IaIIae, q. 23, a. 1.

9. S.T., IaIIae, q. 27, a. 2.

10. S.T., IaIIae, q. 23, a. 1, ad. 2.

11. Reinhold Niebuhr, *The Children of Light and the Children of Darkness* (New York: Charles Scribner's Sons, 1944), p. 189.

12. Arthur C. McGill, *Suffering: A Test of Theological Method* (Philadelphia: The Geneva Press, 1968), p. 47.

13. G. K. Chesterton, *The Everlasting Man* (Garden City, N.Y.: Doubleday Image Books, 1955), p. 227.

14. C. S. Lewis, *The Problem of Pain* (London: Fontana Books, 1957), p. 141.

3. *Friendship and Fidelity*

1. Plutarch, "On Having Many Friends," *Moralia*, II, trans. F. C. Babbott (London: William Heinemann, 1928), 94B (p. 53).

2. Cf. Aristotle, *Nicomachean Ethics*, I, vi, 1096a; and Plato, *Republic*, 595c.

3. Aelred of Rievaulx, *Spiritual Friendship*, trans. Mary Eugenia Laker, S.S.N.D., Cistercian Fathers Series Number

Five (Washington, D.C.: Consortium Press, 1974), II:69.

4. Dorothy L. Sayers, *Unnatural Death* (New York: Avon Boosk, 1968), p. 158.

5. Samuel Johnson, *Essays from the 'Rambler', 'Adventurer', and 'Idler'*, ed. W. J. Bate (New Haven: Yale University Press, 1968), p. 283 (Idler #23). The citations in this paragraph are all taken from this same essay.

6. *Nicomachean Ethics*, trans. Martin Ostwald (Indianapolis: Bobbs-Merrill, 1962), IX, 3.

7. *Laelius De Amicitia*, trans. William Armistead Falconer (Loeb Classical Library No. 154), XXI, 78. Future references will be identified within parentheses in the body of the text.

8. Ralph Waldo Emerson, "Friendship," *Essays and Journals*, selected by Lewis Mumford (Garden City, N.Y.: Doubleday, 1968), p. 169.

9. The same emphasis on the importance of a probationary period appears in Aelred of Rievaulx's *Spiritual Friendship*, the high-water mark of monastic thought about friendship and a treatise heavily dependent on Cicero's *De Amicitia*. In the monastic context, of course, it is not difficult to see this emphasis take institutional shape in the concept of a novitiate.

10. *Spiritual Friendship*, III:52.

11. Søren Kierkegaard, *Works of Love*, trans. Howard and Edna Hong (New York: Harper Torchbooks, 1964), pp. 184f.

12. See Reinhold Niebuhr, *The Nature and Destiny of Man*, vol. II: *Human Destiny* (New York: Charles Scribner's Sons, 1964), p. 69.

4. Politics and Ethics: Civic Friendship

1. J. Glenn Gray, *The Warriors: Reflections on Men in Battle* (New York: Harcourt, Brace and Company, 1959), p. 45.

2. Ibid., p. 95.

3. Cited in R. D. Hicks, *Stoic and Epicurean* (New York: Charles Scribner's Sons, 1910), p. 196.

4. Gray, p. 90.

5. See Stephen G. Salkever, "Freedom, Participation, and Happiness," *Political Theory* 5 (August 1977), 391–413.

6. Michael Walzer, *Obligations: Essays on Disobedience, War, and Citizenship* (New York: Simon and Schuster, 1970), p. 211.

7. Wilson Carey McWilliams, *The Idea of Fraternity in America* (Berkeley: University of California Press, 1973), p. 74.

8. Ibid., pp. 72f.

9. Horst H. Hutter, "Friendship in Theory and Practice: A Study of Greek and Roman Theories of Friendship in Their Social Settings" (Ph.D. diss.: Stanford University, 1972), p. 157. My discussion of the *hetaery* here draws upon Hutter's very interesting and helpful fifth chapter.

10. Ibid., p. 147.

11. Salkever, p. 404.

12. Jean-Jacques Rousseau, *The Social Contract*, trans. Maurice Cranston (New York: Penguin Books, 1968), III, 8.

13. Walzer, p. 186.

14. Ibid., p. 187.

15. Here and at other points in this chapter I draw directly upon my essay, "Understanding the Apathetic Citizen," *Dialog* 17 (Autumn 1978), 303-308.

16. Yves Simon, *Philosophy of Democratic Government* (Chicago: University of Chicago Press, 1951), p. 57.

17. Rousseau, II, 7.

18. Ibid., IV, 8.

19. Martin Hengel, *Victory over Violence: Jesus and the Revolutionists*, trans. David E. Green (Philadelphia: Fortress Press, 1973), p. 2.

20. Reinhold Niebuhr, *The Children of Light and the Children of Darkness* (New York: Charles Scribner's Sons, 1944), p. 5.

21. Epicurus, *Letters, Principal Doctrines and Vatican Sayings*, trans. Russel M. Geer (Indianapolis: Bobbs-Merrill, 1964), Principal Doctrines XXVII and XIV.

22. See Hutter's discussion, pp. 103ff.

23. C. S. Lewis, *The Four Loves* (New York: Harcourt Brace Jovanovich, 1960), pp. 114f.

24. See Hutter, pp. 246ff. Quotations from Cicero's *De Amicitia* are from the Loeb Classical Library edition, trans. William Armistead Falconer.

25. Michel de Montaigne, *Essays*, trans. J. M. Cohen (New

York: Penguin Books, 1958), pp. 98, 101.

26. E. M. Forster, "What I Believe," in *Two Cheers for Democracy* (London: Edward Arnold, Ltd. [1951], rpt. 1972), p. 66.

27. Graham Greene, *The Human Factor* (New York: Avon Books, 1978), p. 211.

28. Ibid., p. 155.

29. Walzer, pp. 21f.

30. Epicurus, Vatican Saying LXXVIII.

31. Lewis, p. 103.

32. Walzer, p. 20.

33. Søren Kierkegaard, *Works of Love,* trans. Howard and Edna Hong (New York: Harper Torchbooks, 1964), p. 80.

34. Ludwic Dugas, *L'Amitié Antique d'après les Moeurs Populaires et les Théories des Philosophes* (Paris: Felix Alcan, 1894), p. 305.

5. *Friendship and Vocation*

1. My thinking on the topic of this chapter was originally stimulated by an essay, to my knowledge still unpublished, by Ralph Potter on friendship and vocation.

2. Kenneth E. Kirk, *The Vision of God: The Christian Doctrine of the Summum Bonum,* abridged edition of the Bampton Lectures for 1928 (Cambridge: James Clarke, 1934), pp. 39f.

3. Einar Billing, *Our Calling,* trans. Conrad Bergendoff (Philadelphia: Fortress Press, 1964), p. 10.

4. Cf. Max Weber, *The Protestant Ethic and the Spirit of Capitalism,* trans. Talcott Parsons (New York: Charles Scribner's Sons, 1958).

5. Michael Walzer, *The Revolution of the Saints: A Study in the Origins of Radical Politics* (New York: Atheneum, 1972), p. 210.

6. "William Perkins on Callings," in *Puritan Political Ideas,* ed. Edmund S. Morgan (Indianapolis: Bobbs-Merrill, 1965), pp. 35-59. Future citations will be given by page number in parentheses within the body of the text.

7. Billing, p. 17.

8. Ibid., p. 29.

9. Weber, pp. 160f.

10. Dorothy L. Sayers, *Gaudy Night* (New York: Avon Books, 1968). All citations will be given by page number in parentheses within the body of the text.

11. *Quadragesimo Anno* (1931), par. 135.

12. Dorothy Sayers, "Why Work?" in *Creed or Chaos* (New York: Harcourt. Brace & Co., 1949), p. 54.

13. *Nicomachean Ethics*, trans. Martin Ostwald (Indianapolis: Bobbs-Merrill, 1962), VIII, 1.

14. P. D. Anthony, *The Ideology of Work* (London: Tavistock Publications, 1977), p. 277.

15. Anthony, p. 304.

16. Karl Marx, "The German Ideology," in *The Marx-Engels Reader*, ed. Robert C. Tucker (New York: W. W. Norton & Company, 1972), p. 114.

17. Anthony, p. 145.

18. Karl Barth, *Church Dogmatics*, III/4 (Edinburgh: T. & T. Clark, 1961), p. 599.

19. John Calvin, *Institutes of the Christian Religion*, Library of Christian Classics, vol. XX, ed. John T. McNeill, trans. Ford Lewis Battles (Philadelphia: Westminster Press, 1960), III, x, 6 (p. 725).

20. Wilson Carey McWilliams, *The Idea of Fraternity in America* (Berkeley: University of California Press, 1973), p. 74.

21. William F. May, "The Sin Against the Friend: Betrayal," *Cross Currents* 17 (1967), 167.

22. I rely here on chapter 15 of Adele M. Fiske's *Friends and Friendship in Monastic Tradition* (Cuernavaca, Mexico: Centro Intercultural de Documentación, 1970). The citations in the paragraphs following come from this chapter. Anselm's concept of friendship is considerably more complicated than my few remarks here can indicate. For further information consult R. W. Southern, *Saint Anselm and His Biographer* (Cambridge University Press, 1963), pp. 67–76; and Brian Patrick McGuire, "Love, friendship and sex in the eleventh century: The experience of Anselm," *Studia Theologica* 28 (1974), 111–152.

23. St. Augustine, *City of God*, trans. Henry Bettenson (New York: Penguin Books, 1972), XIX, 19.

Epilogue

1. Michel de Montaigne, *Essays*, trans. by J. M. Cohen (New York: Penguin Books, 1958), p. 93.
2. Cf. a similar suggestion by C. S. Lewis, *The Four Loves* (New York: Harcourt Brace Jovanovich, 1960), p. 124.

Index

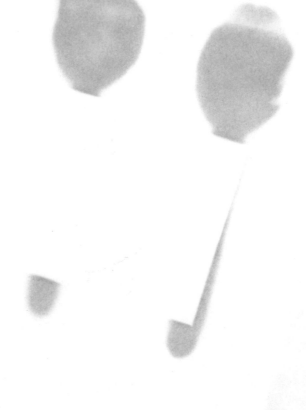